P9-CKN-219

The Book of Ethics

The Book of Ethics

Expert Guidance for Professionals
Who Treat Addiction

Edited by

Cynthia M. A. Geppert, M.D., Ph.D., M.P.H.

and

Laura Weiss Roberts, M.D., M.A.

HAZELDEN®

Hazelden
Center City, Minnesota 55012
hazelden.org

© 2008 by Hazelden Foundation
All rights reserved. Published 2008
Printed in the United States of America

No part of this publication may be reproduced, stored in a retrieval system, or transmitted in any form or by any means—electronic, mechanical, photocopying, recording, scanning, or otherwise—without the express written permission of the publisher. Failure to comply with these terms may expose you to legal action and damages for copyright infringement.

ISBN: 978-1-59285-492-9

Library of Congress Cataloging-in-Publication Data
The book of ethics : expert guidance for professionals who treat addiction / [edited by] Cynthia M. A. Geppert and Laura Weiss Roberts.
    p. ; cm.
  Includes bibliographical references.
  ISBN 978-1-59285-492-9 (softcover)
  1. Substance abuse—Treatment—Moral and ethical aspects. I. Geppert, Cynthia M. A., 1958- II. Roberts, Laura Weiss, 1960-
  [DNLM: 1. Ethics, Clinical. 2. Substance-Related Disorders—therapy. WM 270 B724 2008]
  RC564.B64 2008
  362.29—dc22
                              2008018792

Editor's note
For the sake of convenience and consistency throughout this text, the term "patient" refers to any person who presents at an addiction or mental health care setting for treatment. Some practitioners prefer to refer to these people as clients or individuals.

The names, details, and circumstances may have been changed to protect the privacy of those mentioned in this publication.

This publication is not intended as a substitute for the advice of health care professionals.

Alcoholics Anonymous and AA are registered trademarks of Alcoholics Anonymous World Services, Inc.

12 11 10 09   2 3 4 5 6

Cover design by Theresa Jaeger Gedig
Interior design by Madeline Berglund
Typesetting by Madeline Berglund

"This book delivers on its promise: expert, eminently useable guidance on ethical issues regarding therapeutic relationships; harm reduction; co-occurring disorders; cultural and spiritual considerations; forensics; chronic pain; and issues with women, children, and teens. Through top-notch planning, clear writing, integrated contributions, and attention to practical examples that illustrate the issues and ethical principles woven through the volume, the editors have made a major contribution to the addiction specialty. There is something for everyone here. A welcome, important addition to every addiction counselor's toolbox."

—Howard A. Liddle, Ed.D., ABPP (Family Psychology)
Professor of Epidemiology and Public Health, and Psychology
Director of the Center for Treatment Research on Adolescent Drug Abuse
University of Miami Miller School of Medicine

"I don't know where I've faced more ethical dilemmas—as an institutional review board chairman, an alcohol and drug clinical researcher, or a primary care physician—but I was pleasantly surprised and relieved to find a book that can help us all systematically find the best solutions in areas where there often seem to be no right answers. The take-home message in this book is balance—balancing the many, often competing factors that make applied ethics so challenging."

—Richard Saitz, M.D., M.P.H., F.A.C.P., F.A.S.A.M.
Director of Clinical Addiction Research and Education Unit
Professor of Medicine and Epidemiology
Boston University Schools of Medicine & Public Health and Boston Medical Center

"Geppert, Roberts, and the contributors offer sensitive, wise counsel to effectively work with five ethical principles: autonomy, respect for persons, confidentiality, truth telling, and nonmaleficence. Everyone can benefit from this judicious and compassionate consideration of ethical challenges."

—Robert L. Dupont, M.D.
First Director, National Institute on Drug Abuse (NIDA)
President, Institute for Behavior and Health (IBH), Inc.
Author, *The Selfish Brain: Learning from Addiction*

"A wonderful, easy-to-read, comprehensive examination of the central ethical principles that guide professionals working with addicted individuals and those with co-occurring problems. The authors' recommendations are thoughtful, and the case examples current and provocative. This book gathers an interesting group of authors who offer expertise and thoughts on ethical issues ranging from harm reduction and boundaries with clients to stigma and spirituality. This should be required reading for every addiction professional."

—Carlo C. DiClemente, Professor of Psychology
University of Maryland, Baltimore County

"Professionals who treat addiction span a wide range of perspectives and practices. Some mandate abstinence while others argue for harm reduction. Some view medication with suspicion while others embrace it as an essential option. Whatever your inclination, you will be informed and challenged by this thorough examination of the ethical issues and dilemmas in addictions treatment. *The Book of Ethics* will increase your IQ and fill the gaps between the wide range of perspectives and practices that divide many who treat addictions."

—David Mee-Lee, M.D.
Psychiatrist Certified in Addiction Medicine
Senior Advisor to The Change Companies
DML Training and Consulting

"An important book that should be on the desk of every clinician, and for those pursuing certification or licensure in a variety of specialties dealing with addiction. This book specifically addresses issues of relevance to the treatment of substance abuse, including ethical issues relating to harm reduction, co-occurring disorders, mandated treatment, and the cultural/spiritual dimensions of addictions treatment. Each chapter includes cogent case examples that illustrate the ethical issues and dilemmas."

—Joseph Nowinski, Ph.D.
Supervising Psychologist, University of Connecticut Health Center
Author, *The Twelve Step Facilitation Outpatient Program*

CONTENTS

FIGURES AND TABLES

It has become fashionable among authors of ethics books to tout the timeliness of their work. When said about the content of the present volume, this is anything but cliché. Coalescing scientific, clinical, and social developments make this a relevant, even urgent, and highly salient offering. Every month there are new reports of addictive drugs from clandestine laboratories hitting the streets, joining the age-old scourges of alcohol and tobacco. Even discoveries for severe and chronic pain have been distorted in their misuse to create an epidemic of addiction to novel prescription narcotics.

Policymakers, society, and people with addiction struggle with competing and often conflicting models of addiction, whether seen as disease, crime, personal weakness, genetic determinism, or a hybrid of all the above. At the heart of these contemporary debates are ethical questions as ancient as philosophy: free will versus responsibility, choice versus determinism, treatment versus punishment. But a modern understanding and a new paradigm for care are now possible. Emerging neurobiological evidence illuminates the circuits and transmitters involved in craving and reward, dependence and withdrawal, and the genetic precursors to addiction itself. With greater understanding of the biological basis of addiction and substance use disorders, we may now begin to make some progress in this field, particularly from an ethical perspective.

No one confronts these questions with as much immediacy and poignancy as addiction professionals, who daily face complex ethical dilemmas regarding issues of confidentiality, consent, and the balance of harm and benefit. These questions affect clients and their families but also society as a whole. Although, as this volume shows, law often provides the framework in which these decisions can be made, legal requirements and regulations do not provide trim and tidy packaged solutions to the ethical problems of caring for people with substance use disorders. Nor can the present volume offer such ready-made answers.

What this book on addiction ethics does provide is general guidance and guidelines on key issues stemming from the accumulated wisdom of a group of clinician-educators and researchers with extensive experience and diverse expertise in the addictions field. This text also presents emerging controversies and novel, as yet untested ideas around age-old questions in the care of people with addictions. For this reason, we offer this work modestly in the hope that it will stir new thinking and opportunities to substantiate (or not) these claims. Addiction is a rapidly evolving field of clinical science and one in which consensus on many questions has not yet been established. Thus, this book, as the work of many expert authors, represents innovative thinking and in some instances even contradictory views.

It is incumbent upon all authors (but particularly those who are also ethicists) to give credit where credit is due. In this case we wish to acknowledge LeClair Bissell and James E. Royce's pioneering volume *Ethics for Addiction Professionals,* first published by Hazelden in 1987. Building on this and other sources cited in the book, the authors strive to expand the humanistic and clinically oriented approach to addiction ethics to a host of new stakeholders and issues that have arisen since the earlier volume was published. *The Book of Ethics: Expert Guidance for Professionals Who Treat Addiction* explores new territory in discussing the specific ethical concerns involved in treating women, children and adolescents, and patients with dual diagnoses. The emerging consensus regarding the importance of recognizing cultural and spiritual aspects in caring for patients with addiction is addressed in these pages, as is the more controversial role of harm reduction in therapy for substance use disorders.

The Book of Ethics also attends to the ethical ground of clinical work by introducing addiction professionals from all disciplines to the fundamental principles and practices of modern clinical ethics, such as informed consent, confidentiality, and scare resource allocation. Forensic concerns—so prevalent in all of mental health treatment—are presented, as are the parameters of the therapeutic relationship with adaptation and adoption for the field of addictions.

Perhaps no illness has resulted in as much tragedy for patients, families, and health care professionals as addictions have. Fortunately, emerging pharmacological and behavioral treatments offer hope for sustained recovery for millions of people for whom even five years ago there were far fewer options. Yet with these new therapies, experience has shown us, will come new ethical dilemmas that will require ethically informed and clinically skilled addiction professionals who can address these challenges for the good of the patient and the culture. It is to facilitate this honorable effort that we have written this text, and we trust it will serve those navigating this ever-more-complex landscape of addictions as a worthy compass.

C. G. and *L. R.*

ACKNOWLEDGMENTS

I would like to thank first and foremost my coeditor and co-author, Dr. Laura Roberts, who has been my mentor, teacher, friend, and inspiration for over a decade. Without Dr. Roberts's enduring encouragement and wise guidance, my career and this book would not have been possible. I would also like to express my gratitude to Dr. Michael Bogenschutz, who has been a colleague, coauthor, and mentor in the field of addictions during my residency and beyond. My gratitude is also extended to those many colleagues and teachers, students, and residents too numerous to mention who have contributed directly and indirectly to the spirit of this book, chief among them Drs. John Gluck, Stephen Lewis, Jeffrey Katzman, and Lane Leckman, as well as all our gifted coauthors. My deepest love and thanks to my eighty-seven-year-old retired nurse mother, Ann, for her unconditional support for this work and through all the defeats and victories of my life and to Kira, my ever faithful Akita. Finally, but most meaningfully, I would like to express my respect and compassion for the deep suffering that patients and families struggling with psychiatric illness and addiction daily experience. It is our privilege as clinicians and ethicists to participate in their care and decision making in a collaborative spirit of recovery.

C. G.

My heartfelt appreciation goes to my patients and to all people living with substance use disorders and mental illnesses. I am awed by their humanity, courage, and authenticity. They suffer immensely and yet, in sharing their experiences and inviting us into their lives, they give so very much to us. It is our debt. I sincerely thank Dr. Cynthia Geppert, my partner in this creative project. Our collaboration on many projects over many years has been among the greatest privileges of my career. Dr. Geppert does meaningful and valuable work—and as with all brilliant students, she has taught her teachers brilliantly. I thank my friends Teresita, John, Doug, Cathryn, and Andy for their kindness, support, and the generous gift of their time. I wish to acknowledge, with affection, my babies, Madeline, Helen, Willa, and Tom. They are loved, loving, lovely young people who seem to dish up the rich, sweet goodness of life like ice cream. I am grateful to know them.

L. R.

Together, we wish to thank the editors at Hazelden: Richard Solly for never giving up on this project and Jodie Carter for seeing it through. We also wish to thank Ann Tennier, who was indefatigable and gifted in her job as our editorial assistant.

C. G. and *L. R.*

Ethical Foundations of Substance Abuse Treatment

CYNTHIA M. A. GEPPERT, M.D., PH.D., M.P.H.
LAURA WEISS ROBERTS, M.D., M.A.

Substance abuse affects all of us, and the personal and societal costs of substance-related disorders are both real and significant. One in six individuals in the United States experiences addiction over the course of his or her lifetime (Kessler et al. 2005). The burden of addiction is amplified when one considers the people who love, live with, and work with individuals with addiction. Health professionals—irrespective of specialty or discipline—will encounter consequences of substance abuse in their clinical work. Caring for patients with the complex issues that accompany addiction creates many challenges: biological, psychological, social, spiritual—and ethical. Whether indirectly, through the societal costs of alcohol or other drug use, or more directly, through contact with an individual suffering with these conditions, the burdens are great.

Pervasiveness of Substance Abuse

Addiction is a wide and deep public health problem in the United States. The 2007 National Survey on Drug Use and Health found that an estimated 22.6 million people—an alarming 9.2 percent of the U.S. population—met the criteria for either substance abuse or dependence in 2006. This survey reports that 3.2 million people abused or were dependent on alcohol and illicit drugs. An additional 3.8 million misused or were dependent on drugs alone, and 15.6 million abused or were dependent on alcohol alone.

Approximately one-quarter of all mortality in the United States can be attributed to alcohol and drugs. During 2001 there were 75,766 alcohol-attributable deaths and 2.3 million years of potential life lost, or 30 years of life on average, per death related to alcohol (Substance Abuse and Mental Health Services Administration 2006). Addiction accounts for 40 million illnesses and injuries each year and over $400 billion in health care costs, lost productivity, and crime (McGinnis and Foege 1999).

Psychological distress was strongly associated with the use of substances in this National Survey on Drug Use and Health, with 22.3 million adults reporting both serious mental health problems and abuse or dependence on drugs or alcohol, compared with a 7.7 percent rate of abuse or dependence for those who did not report psychological distress (Substance Abuse and Mental Health Services Administration 2007a). The Centers for Disease Control and Prevention (CDC) estimates that excessive alcohol consumption is the third-leading cause of preventable death, with fatal consequences from cirrhosis, cancer, domestic violence, and motor vehicle crashes, among others (Centers for Disease Control and Prevention 2004).

While the human toll of addiction is immeasurable, the economic price is also striking, at $180.9 billion related to drug abuse in 2002. This figure encompasses both the use of health care resources and the ramifications of crime, along with loss of potential productivity from disability, death, and withdrawal from the workforce (Lewin Group 2004).

People living with addictions in this country receive little in the way of substance-related health care. Only 2.5 million of the 23 million persons with substance abuse or dependence in the United States received treatment at a specialty facility in 2006. Indeed, it appears that most treatment for addiction-related illness in the United States is managed in acute care settings such as emergency departments (Substance Abuse and Mental Health Services Administration 2007a). The Drug Abuse Warning Network provides data regarding emergency department visits involving illicit drugs, alcohol, or the nonmedical use of prescription medications. In 2005, the latest date for which a report is available, there were 1,449,154 visits for abuse of substances. The majority of these visits resulted from a combination of drugs and alcohol, and there was a 21 percent increase since 2004 in the misuse or abuse of pharmaceuticals (Substance Abuse and Mental Health Services Administration 2007b).

In 2006, 940,000 persons reported feeling that they needed treatment for an illicit drug or alcohol use problem, but 625,000 of these individuals made no effort to obtain treatment. This underscores that education, outreach, and an increase in services are desperately needed if the health care community is to address this public health crisis (Substance Abuse and Mental Health Services Administration 2007a).

This lack of engagement in treatment is itself a symptom of addiction, which adversely affects the mind, the will, and the emotions. Persons with a serious substance abuse problem often lack insight into their own disorders and are not fully aware of the havoc that addiction is wreaking on their health, families, careers, and community. The exercise of poor judgment, obsessive efforts to obtain the substance, and compulsive prioritizing of intoxication with drugs or alcohol over other values are integral aspects of addiction that endanger the individual and may harm relatives, friends, and even strangers.

The Moral and Ethical Salience of Living with Addictions

The distinct nature of substance misuse—for its specific biological, psychological, social, and spiritual consequences—renders it intrinsically and ineluctably moral. Caring for people living with addictions thus requires a high standard of ethical knowledge and professional skill. Substance use disorders are highly stigmatized and hence require more rigorous confidentiality protections than do other medical conditions. Addiction often involves illicit drugs, high-risk behaviors (including suicidal and homicidal ideas and impulses), and other actions that intersect with the law (such as criminal conduct), making it imperative that addiction professionals understand their professional and legal obligations and how these impact the therapeutic alliance.

Because persons with substance abuse or dependence often have cognitive and volitional impairments and are frequently subject to coercion to enter treatment from employers, families, the courts, and health care providers, scrupulous attention to full and authentic informed patient consent is highly salient.

Several issues may complicate the therapeutic relationship. Clinicians may have internalized cultural biases and personal prejudices regarding addiction. Moreover, many health care providers involved in addiction treatment may themselves be in recovery. This special aspect of addiction therapy will require self-awareness, frequent consultation, and monitoring of therapeutic boundaries for the well-being of both patient and professional. Finally, as opposed to other areas of health care and biomedicine, clinical ethics in relation to addiction and co-occurring conditions is comparatively underdeveloped, with little research and education focused on the topic (Walker et al. 2005).

Ethics in Health Care

Ethics is the branch of philosophy that describes values related to human conduct and explores what is right and wrong about certain actions and decisions. Historically, those involved in the law, the clergy, and medicine have been granted a substantial measure of self-governance in return for their pledge to observe explicit and agreed-upon ethical standards. This places the well-being and interests of the client or patient above all other interests that may encroach upon the situation, whether personal, economic, or political. The professional ethics of health care practitioners, including addiction professionals, is often called medical ethics.

Many recognize the origin of medical ethics in the Hippocratic School of 200 B.C. The duties expressed in the famous Oath of the Hippocratic School, such as confidentiality, nonmaleficence, and beneficence, remain fundamental principles of modern health care. Other core concepts of contemporary bioethics in the United States, such as autonomy and respect for persons, emerged in response to the rise of technology in medical practice, evolving appreciation of ethical issues in human research, and the larger human rights movement. The specialty of addiction treatment, which includes physicians, psychologists, social workers, licensed addiction counselors, and other health care disciplines, is relatively new and intrinsically multidisciplinary. Thus, the ethical codes of each type of practitioner will have specific emphases, yet all share the commitment to the essential ethical principles and virtues discussed in this chapter.

Ethical Principles

Ethical principles are general standards or maxims that guide ethical reasoning and conduct. Principles reflect an expert consensus on ethical priorities and values that frames ethical decision making in clinical care. Principles are sometimes also called rules or laws and, when applied to specific clinical cases, indicate broadly what decisions and actions may be ethically acceptable or justifiable. Closely related and often overlapping with principles are virtues such as compassion and honesty. Principles are a form of knowledge or reasoning, while virtues are habitual qualities of a person's character that incline him or her to choose the good and do what is right.

The principles of respect for persons, autonomy, compassion, confidentiality, privacy, truth telling, nonmaleficence, and beneficence form a necessary foundation for clinicians who treat patients with substance abuse or dependence. To be effective, professionals caring for individuals with addictions will ideally embody the virtuous dispositions of altruism and fidelity, among others, if they are to internalize and integrate the cognitive principles into their practice. The following principles and their application to addiction treatment are summarized in Table 1.1, Application of Ethical Principles to Addiction.

Respect for Persons

Respect for persons is the idea that every individual is endowed with dignity and worth, no matter what his or her ethnicity, income, social status, sexual orientation, cognitive function, judicial standing, or diagnoses. Substance abuse clinicians will find some of their greatest ethical challenges in facing both internalized prejudices against their patients and, even more, cultural and organizational discrimination.

Autonomy

Autonomy, or self-determination, has its origin in the concept of respect for persons and is arguably the overriding principle in U.S. medical ethics. It is inculcated in Anglo-American law and instantiated in health care chiefly through the practices of informed consent and confidentiality. "Autonomy" literally means "self-rule" and is the right and ability to make one's own decisions—in the present context, decisions related to health care in general and addiction treatment specifically.

Addiction professionals who work with diverse populations and patients across the life cycle recognize that not all cultures or generations unilaterally or uniformly endorse autonomy in its individual form. For many cultures, and among some older persons, respect for authority is not tantamount to paternalism, and the family or community is the locus of decision making (Carrese and Rhodes 1995).

Compassion

The Latin source for the word "compassion" means "to suffer with" and is closely related to empathy, "feeling with." Sympathy, which is literally "feeling for," is a reaction characterized more by distance and pity than compassion, which is an active involvement to relieve another's distress.

Confidentiality

Confidentiality requires that the clinician not disclose information obtained in the treatment relationship to third parties (unless required by law) without the consent of the patient. Because confidentiality is constrained by law, it is regarded as a privilege (i.e., not an inherent "right"). Although confidentiality is important in all of medical ethics, the stigma and criminal charges connected to the abuse of alcohol and drugs in our society make confidentiality of vital significance to addiction professionals.

Privacy

Closely related to, but distinct from, confidentiality is the right of privacy. Privacy is defined as the right to be free from intrusions into one's physical body, space, mind, and personal information.

Truth Telling

Also closely related to confidentiality is the obligation to be honest. Truth telling includes the positive duty to tell the truth and the negative duty not to mislead others. Truth telling requires clinicians to fully and accurately disclose health information to patients and their surrogates on the basis of informed consent and simultaneously to avoid misrepresenting such information to or withholding it from those who have a legitimate claim to receive it. Perhaps the most complicated and agonizing ethical conflicts substance-use clinicians will confront are those related to confidentiality and truth telling, such as mandatory reporting of pregnant women living with addictions in some jurisdictions (Roberts and Dunn 2003).

Nonmaleficence

Nonmaleficence is the ethical duty to "do no harm." The protean and pervasive damage of addiction gives, some say, this principle of nonmaleficence the greatest weight in the ethics of addiction treatment.

A related concept is that of harm reduction—that is, creating treatments that help minimize the burdens associated with disease. Harm reduction, despite some detractors, is rationalized as a valid and valuable form of treatment because of the devastating consequences of addiction. This is especially true because, contrary to much popular and even professional opinion, there are effective treatments, both established psychosocial interventions, like cognitive-behavioral and contingency modalities, and emerging and unprecedented pharmacological therapies, like those for alcohol and opioid dependence (Rawson et al. 2002). Thus harm reduction is possible and therefore creates its own ethical imperative, in the eyes of many. See Chapter 3 for more information on the harm reduction approach.

Beneficence

Beneficence is the ethical duty to seek to do good—to bring about benefits to individual patients and, many would argue, improve conditions in society as well. The efficacy of addiction treatments in real-world clinical settings enables substance abuse clinicians to practice beneficence to an extent not previously achievable. Addiction clinicians in the twenty-first century can have the same confidence in their abilities to do good for their patients and the same hope for their patients' participation in, and response to, treatment as providers treating other chronic medical illnesses, such as hypertension and diabetes (McLellan et al. 2000).

Ethical Decision Making

Addiction, particularly in the United States, is a complex phenomenon, with history and meanings beyond the clinical realm. The social, political, and cultural associations of addiction often intensify the ethical dilemmas shared with other forms of medical treatment and extend the ethical questions into legal, public policy, and even spiritual spheres (Room 2006). Four ethical aspects of addiction—stigma, legal implications, voluntarism, and justice—specifically affect a clinician's ethical decision making to a greater degree than perhaps any other area of health care.

Stigma

The first, and most powerful, aspect of addiction is stigma. "Stigma" literally means "branding or labeling." This term connotes disgrace or diminishment of the person by virtue of some attribute or characteristic. For persons with addiction, stigma plays out in diverse ways—nuances of what is said or not said at one end of the spectrum to social rejection, loss of or inability to obtain employment or insurance, alienation from family and friends, political marginalization, and other forms of subtle and overt discrimination (Roberts and Dunn 2003).

TABLE 1.1

Application of Ethical Principles to Addiction

Ethical Principle	Example of Dilemma
Autonomy	A patient diagnosed with problem drinking by his primary care provider refuses referral to a substance abuse counselor.
Respect for persons	An addiction psychiatrist is treating an HIV-positive, homeless sex worker for amphetamine dependence in his private practice. His staff members tell the doctor they should not have to treat this kind of patient.
Confidentiality	A counselor in a substance abuse program is asked by a patient she is seeing for alcohol dependence to not tell the psychologist (who is the counselor's supervisor) that the patient is suicidal.
Truth telling	A patient in an outpatient substance abuse program asks the psychologist working there to not report a toxicology screen positive for opioids to her probation officer.
Nonmaleficence	A psychiatrist is treating a patient who has a history of cocaine dependence in remission and has developed chronic back pain. The primary care provider asks if it is safe to prescribe opioids to the patient.
Beneficence	A social worker exerts considerable effort to arrange housing for a homeless patient recovering from opioid dependence. The patient then is threatened with eviction for allowing drug-using friends to stay in his apartment.

Many studies demonstrate the powerful impact of stigma on people with substance-related conditions. Studies of medical students and physicians suggest that stigma is associated with substance use and may discourage appropriate care-seeking as well as lead colleagues to "collude" with impaired peers to prevent their discovery (Roberts et al. 2001). For example, in a study of 1,027 medical students at nine training institutions, researchers found that 47 percent endorsed having concern about at least one mental health or substance-related condition and that concern about confidentiality and stigma discouraged them from obtaining appropriate care. Students were concerned that they would be jeopardized academically if they sought treatment. Moreover, most students would remain silent even if they suspected life-threatening substance abuse problems in another student.

In a second study conducted with 107 multidisciplinary clinicians in Alaska and New Mexico, researchers found that caregivers were reluctant to talk about alcohol abuse, mental health, drug abuse, and sexual life issues with their personal caregivers. For more stigmatizing conditions or issues, these clinicians preferred to avoid or delay necessary care or to go to other cities for treatment (Roberts et al. 2003).

In a third study, which took place in 2006, 197 patients in fifteen residential and outpatient substance abuse treatment facilities reported that the participants experienced high levels of enacted stigma, perceived stigma, and even self-stigma related to substance abuse. Most disturbing, the patients reported that the treatment system itself stigmatized people in recovery (Luoma et al. 2006).

Legal Implications

A second and distinct aspect of addiction is its legal implications. Although the law is often a considerable factor in medical decision making, in no other area does it weigh as heavily as in substance use treatment, where stimulants, opioids, and marijuana remain illegal drugs and where alcohol use too often involves charges of driving while intoxicated. Consider that among the 3.7 million adults on probation in 2000, 24.2 percent reported using an illicit drug in the month prior to the survey, compared with 5.5 percent of adults not on probation. The Federal Bureau of Justice reported that two-thirds of victims of violence from a spouse or partner stated that the perpetrator had been drinking, in contrast to one-third of victims whose attackers were strangers. Similarly, the Substance Abuse and Mental Health Services Administration (SAMHSA) found that children of parents with addictions were nearly three times more likely to be abused and four times more commonly neglected than children of parents who did not abuse substances (Stone 2000).

These and other grim statistics imply that most clinicians working in substance abuse treatment will routinely encounter ethical conflicts with the law, such as how to manage a positive "tox screen" in a patient who is on parole or alcohol-impaired driving by a patient in an intensive outpatient treatment program.

Voluntarism

The third aspect of addiction is that drugs and alcohol negatively affect the self-determination and voluntarism that are requisite for self-knowledge, careful and intentional conduct needed for moral responsibility and social accountability. Increasing evidence from the neurosciences indicates that the longer and heavier an addictive substance is used, the more probable it is for the user to be impulsive and unable to forgo short-term rewards for long-term gains (Vuchinich and Simpson 1998). Neurobiology is elucidating the role of genetics, the neuro-circuits, and endocrine stress responses in vulnerability to addiction and the long-term potentiation involved in the craving and cueing that drive compulsive use and relapse (Weiss 2005). Although few experts would say that even a severe and chronic substance-abusing individual is without legal culpability or completely unable to stop using substances, many thoughtful researchers and ethicists are examining the implications of these impairments for decisional capacity, informed consent, refusal of care, and even for mandated or coerced treatment of addictions (Caplan 2006).

Justice

The fourth and final distinguishing aspect of addiction ethics is the enormous treatment gap, which has professional and public policy implications. Lack of parity in funding for mental health treatment, including addictions, represents a substantial health disparity in the U.S. system of medical care. Indeed an overwhelming majority of persons who struggle with addiction also have other disadvantages. Ethnic, economic, social, and cultural backgrounds and medical and psychiatric comorbidities all compound one's status in an underserved group. For this reason, we have argued that people with addictions have overlapping sources of vulnerability when seeking health care resources. In the 2005 National Survey on Drug Use and Health, 23.2 million Americans age twelve and older needed treatment for a drug or alcohol problem, but only 2.3 million received treatment at a facility specializing in addictions. This amounts to nearly 21 million individuals who did not obtain treatment for their substance abuse disorder. Even more ethically relevant, of those who received treatment at a specialty facility, 45 percent paid for it out of their own income or savings (Substance Abuse and Mental Health Services Administration 2006). Issues of social justice and fairness related to the lack of parity for treatment of substance use disorders can develop into ethical dilemmas for addiction practitioners regarding accuracy and veracity in documentation and medical record keeping and truth telling to third parties such as insurance companies or employers.

Ethical Dilemmas

An ethical dilemma is a situation in which a person is faced with one or more ethical obligations that cannot be fulfilled equally or at the same time. The choices are generally good and valuable, such as wanting to honor the confidentiality of a suicidal patient while also wishing to protect him or her from self-harm.

The first step in resolving an ethical dilemma is to recognize it as a true moral conflict rather than a legal question, clinical problem,

FIGURE 1.1

Ethical Decision Making

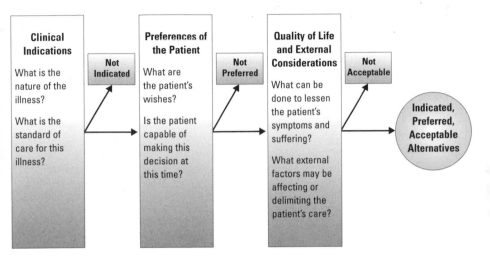

Adapted from Roberts and Dyer (2004: 307).

or institutional matter, all of which have somewhat different approaches and resources for their respective management. Clinicians can improve their understanding of ethical dilemmas by reading articles and books on ethics; obtaining continuing education credits in ethics, which are now required in several addiction disciplines; seeking supervision from clinicians with more experience and wisdom; and consulting with ethics consultants, ethics committees, attorneys, or professional associations.

The second step in dilemma resolution is to analyze the situation in a deliberate and systematic fashion, just as would be done with a clinical case. The National Center for Ethics in Health Care of the Veterans Administration has adapted the widely used model of Jonsen, Siegler, and Winslade (1998) into an even more practical approach to ethical decision making in clinical care. This approach examines three factors: (1) the medical facts involved in a case, (2) the patient's preferences for treatment, and (3) the interests of other parties.

The qualities of good ethical decision making require that the process, justifications, and actual decisions are legally permissible, clinically appropriate and ethically acceptable, and, most important, represent patient-centered care. A practical example of how this approach can be employed can be found in Table 1.2, Case Illustration: A Model for Ethical Decision Making. This table demonstrates the primary factors that should be considered— including medical facts, patient preferences, and the interests of other parties—and that affect a clinician's ethical decision making. Consider the ethical question about whether to report (or not to report), for example, a forty-five-year-old female airline pilot with twenty years of alcohol dependence. This pilot has chosen to drink and to fly, placing passengers and the general public in jeopardy. Given the priority of the flying public, the most ethically appropriate decision will protect the public while also attempting to respect the patient's preferences. For instance, the clinician in this case could try to persuade the pilot to disclose her drinking problem to the airline and advocate for a treatment plan that would allow her to return to flying at an appropriate time in the future (once she is sober for a specified period of time). However, if persuasion is unsuccessful, the good of the public requires that the pilot be reported.

Using a model like the one shown in Table 1.2 helps organize the elements of the dilemma, making it easier to see that there may be a range of ethically justifiable actions (whereas before the analysis, there appeared to be only unacceptable or conflicting options). The most appropriate decisions will share certain characteristics of being clinically sound, legally permissible, ethically balanced, and respectful of a patient's values whenever possible. For instance, refusing to treat a patient's hypertension because it is at least partially due to alcohol use would not be good medical judgment on the part of the practitioner. The most preferable decisions are those that balance the major ethical principles involved within the specific context at hand, rather than weighing one ethical principle more heavily due to subjective considerations by the clinician.

TABLE 1.2

Case Illustration: A Model for Ethical Decision Making

Factor	Case
Medical facts • Diagnoses • Treatment history • Comorbidity • Prognoses	• The patient is a forty-five-year-old pilot with twenty years of alcohol dependence. • She has been drinking two mixed drinks a night and up to five drinks in one sitting several times a month, even when she is scheduled to fly the next day. • She has hypertension and evidence of liver disease, both attributed to alcohol.
Patient preferences • Informed consent • Decisional capacity • Surrogate decision makers	• She wants to attend AA regularly because it is anonymous. • She is willing to try acamprosate, a medication that may reduce drinking. • She does not wish to enter any formal substance use treatment program because she fears her employer, who pays her health insurance, will find out.
Interests of other parties • Family • Health care providers • Employers • Public	• She may lose her job, affecting her partner and two children, if she is reported to the airline. • If she is reported, she may leave treatment and drink even more heavily. • The airline may have an employee assistance program that deals with addiction. • The public is in danger when she flies after drinking because she may be impaired. • The provider has an ethical obligation to protect patient confidentiality and public safety.

Once the clinician understands the advantages and disadvantages of different decision options, the clinician's ethical knowledge base, skills, and consultation network can be employed to review and vet the decision. Another benefit of adopting a structured, consultative means of resolving ethical dilemmas is that it aids in accurate and clear documentation of the clinician's thinking, which is crucial in responding to legal, institutional, or professional issues pertaining to the case.

Confidentiality, Truth Telling, and Clinical Practice

Confidentiality and truth-telling issues are among the most common, complex, and challenging ethical dilemmas addiction professionals confront in their daily practice. The principle of confidentiality is one of the most ancient in professional ethical codes, dating back to the Oath of Hippocrates, which states, "Whatever I see or hear, professionally or privately, which ought not to be divulged, I will keep secret and tell no one" (Lloyd 1983). The modern definition of confidentiality retains the essence of the oath, that information disclosed to a health care professional in the course of a therapeutic relationship should not be disclosed to other parties without the patient's permission unless required by law. Although technological innovations like cellular phones and the Internet, and system changes such as managed care and revisions in federal regulations have all eroded traditional confidentiality protections in most of health care, addiction treatment retains some of the strongest safeguards for patient information (Appelbaum 2002).

The rationale for more robust confidentiality protections in addiction treatment than in other forms of medical care lies in the greater stigma attached to substance use disorders. Only in a confidential setting can patients discuss sensitive, painful, and often stigmatized concerns such as sexual practice, drug and alcohol use, and homicidal or suicidal impulses. Unless patients are assured that their private disclosures to their practitioner will not be used to their detriment through loss of insurance or employment, criminal action, or family conflicts, they will not provide the open, full, and detailed information regarding symptoms and lifestyle necessary for accurate diagnosis and effective treatment. Patients with addictive disorders may be so fearful that their personal health information will be exploited that they may not even come for treatment, resulting in late diagnosis, self-medication, and unnecessary morbidity and mortality.

Adolescents with addictions and women of reproductive age with addictions are two groups in which these tensions between need for treatment and protection of privacy become particularly poignant and complicated (Roberts and Dunn 2003). A study in the *Journal of the American Medical Association* anonymously surveyed 1,295 high school students, and 25 percent said they would not seek help for a health care problem if they knew their parents would be informed. Even among those students who had an established relationship with a provider, 86 percent would seek help for a medical problem, but only 57 percent for a substance abuse issue. Unfortunately, only one-third of respondents were aware of confidentiality safeguards for specific health concerns (Cheng et al. 1993). Specific confidentiality concerns that can arise when treating women are addressed in Chapter 7 and concerns regarding children and adolescents are addressed in Chapter 8.

Closely aligned to the duty of addiction professionals to protect patient information is their obligation to tell patients and others legitimately involved in care the truth regarding their diagnosis, prognosis, and treatment options and the adverse clinical, social, and even legal consequences of continuing to use substances of abuse. Truth telling encompasses the obligation not to deceive patients or others with valid rights to information, such as surrogates and colleagues, and the duty to present scientifically accurate clinical data in a manner that is respectful, nonjudgmental, and empathetic. Clinicians who avoid discussing substance use for fear of alienating a patient or because they do not consider it an appropriate medical issue do a disservice as much as practitioners who are confrontational, stigmatizing, and rejecting (Miller et al. 2001).

Legal Considerations

Legal requirements may shape or at times largely dictate ethical and clinical responsibilities. Although many times respect for the law, good patient care, and ethical practice coincide, there are instances in which they are at odds. It is incumbent upon addiction professionals to possess a working knowledge of the federal and state statutes and regulations applicable to their practice environment and discipline and to have access to competent legal and ethical counsel. See Table 1.3, Key Confidentiality Regulations, for a list of the key confidentiality regulations.

The two federal regulations listed in Table 1.3 take precedence over every other federal, state, or local policy regulation and mandate the circumstances and conditions under which information pertaining to addictions treatment may be disclosed. The following general points provide an outline of the implications of these regulations for clinical care (Brooks 2005).

- The regulations apply to any program that specializes, in whole or in part, in providing substance use disorder assessment, diagnosis, counseling, treatment, or referral and that receives federal assistance, such as any government funding or tax-exempt status.

- The regulations do not allow health information, either written or oral, to be disclosed about any patient who has

TABLE 1.3

Key Confidentiality Regulations

- Confidentiality of Alcohol and Drug Abuse Patient Records, Part 2 of Title 42 (Public Health) of the Code of Federal Regulations (CFR).
- Health Insurance Portability and Accountability Act of 1996 (HIPAA), Parts 160 and 164 of Title 45 (Public Welfare) of the Code of Federal Regulations.
- Applicable state law.

applied for future treatment, who has received treatment in the past, or who is currently in treatment unless the patient has consented to the release or in the case of specific exceptions detailed below.

- The regulations apply to patients who are committed involuntarily or mandated to treatment by the criminal justice system.

- The regulations pertain to any data identifying the patient as having a substance use disorder directly or indirectly from the point the patient makes an appointment.

- The regulations are applicable even if the party requesting the information already possesses it from another source, presents a warrant or subpoena, or has other official status.

- Disclosures are permitted if a patient has signed a valid consent form, but such information cannot be used to criminally investigate or prosecute the patient without a special court order.

For addiction clinicians and programs, the strictest rule usually takes precedence (Clark and Brooks 2003). However there are instances in which there may be conflicts between the regulations themselves or state law beyond the scope of this introductory chapter. For this reason it is important for practitioners to have a working knowledge of the local applicable laws and access to good legal counsel and the privacy officer responsible for confidentiality protections at their practice setting.

The relevance of the statutes in terms of the six general key provisions that each regulation affirms—autonomy, respect for persons, confidentiality, truth telling, nonmaleficence, and beneficence—is what is most important for clinicians to understand.

Clinical Considerations

Faced with the tightness of these regulations and the fact that programs found in violation of the provisions can be fined heavily for breaches, addiction professionals may feel seriously constrained in their ability to obtain the collateral information vital to comprehensive addiction treatment, to arrange mental health treatment, to provide medical care for patients with comorbidities, and to manage any emergencies. Clinical common sense, some basic guidelines for handling confidential information, and an understanding of the available exceptions to disclosure can assist the addiction professional in handling most ethical conundrums. For more difficult cases, appropriate legal consultation should be obtained.

Clinicians ideally will inform substance use disorder clients of confidentiality protections and limitations as soon as they enter treatment and explain the importance of both safeguarding information that could be stigmatizing and obtaining consultations and collateral reports that may improve care. Substance use professionals also must always inform patients about the specific circumstances in which confidentiality protections do not apply. These circumstances—child abuse, infectious diseases, suicide or homicide, and crimes committed against staff, among others— are listed in Table 1.4, General Exceptions to Confidentiality Regulations.

All state laws mandate reporting of certain infectious diseases, such as tuberculosis and sexually transmitted diseases, to public health authorities. Every state has laws that require health care professionals to report suspected child abuse; this exception pertains only to the initial reporting and not to follow-up requests for information, whether in the context of civil or criminal action.

The "duty to warn" is based on an extension of the 1974 *Tarasoff* case in California in which a therapist treating a graduate student failed to warn an identifiable victim whom the student threatened to murder and subsequently killed. Both a duty to warn and to protect emerged from these rulings, which can be discharged through warning a victim, notifying law enforcement, or hospitalizing or otherwise intervening clinically to reduce or

TABLE 1.4

General Exceptions to Confidentiality Regulations

- Patient consent in accordance with the specified form and requirements of the regulations (however, this information may not be used in a criminal investigation or prosecution of a patient without special court order)
- Infectious diseases
- Child abuse
- Suicide and homicide
- Medical emergencies
- Patient information that does not disclose that the patient has a substance use disorder
- Disclosure under special court order
- Staff communications within a program
- Communication with an outside entity that provided support to the program
- Appropriately authorized research, auditing, or evaluation
- Disclosure to a qualified service organization assisting program
- Crimes committed on program premises or against staff members

eliminate the threat (Felthous 1993). Even in states without *Tarasoff*-type legislation, it is understood that there may be a clear professional and moral obligation to warn potential victims of violence if the victim is identifiable, the threat is feasible and imminent, and the warning has a realistic chance of preventing harm. It should be noted that when fulfilling the duty to warn and protect, the clinician should, whenever possible, honor confidentiality safeguards that require that the identity of individuals using substances or in treatment not be disclosed to law enforcement or even the victim.

When in high-risk physical situations (for instance, a patient threatens a staff member or commits a crime on program grounds), the law allows program staff to report the crime to law

Cynthia M. A. Geppert, M.D., Ph.D., M.P.H. ▪ Laura Weiss Roberts, M.D., M.A.

enforcement and to disclose the identifying information about the client, including status in a substance use disorder program. This authorization does not extend to admission of past crimes, even those crimes that are unsolved. Information necessary to treat a patient in a medical emergency that immediately threatens the patient's life can and should always be disclosed to medical staff, even when it involves data about a patient's substance use disorder, such as a patient using cocaine who presents to a local hospital with chest pain and no cardiac history. Those disclosing the information must document the circumstances surrounding the disclosure. To facilitate treatment, addiction professionals within a single program may communicate with one another, for instance, when a patient is transferred from an outpatient to a residential setting. Communications are also permitted with data processing or billing agencies that manage patient records on behalf of a substance use disorder program, with the caveat that these entities agree to abide by the regnant confidentiality regulations, including not releasing the information to a third party without consent (Center for Substance Abuse Treatment 1994).

It is a useful standard for all disclosures or requests for information for other collateral or referral sources, such as family members, employers, or other clinicians, to only reveal the type and quantity of information that is necessary to answer the specific query. This rule holds even when communications are made with patient consent, such as when an addiction treatment counselor is seeking or providing reports to a mental health provider who is treating the counselor's alcohol-dependent patient for co-occurring depression. The request should be limited to information directly related to the mood disorder and include a caution to the other party that he or she is bound by the confidentiality restrictions as well. This norm is particularly important when communicating with insurance companies, employers, or criminal justice officials, who have particular interests, which may not always coincide with the concerns and goals of the patient.

Conflicts between Confidentiality and Truth Telling

Providers caring for patients with substance use disorders all too frequently experience a conflict between protecting patient privacy and autonomy and preventing harm to others. The patient who appears intoxicated at the program or health care facility should be provided with an opportunity to sober up or given safe transportation home. The patient who continues to drive while intoxicated despite counseling and warning is best reported to the state motor vehicle department (in those jurisdictions that allow providers to do so) as being impaired without disclosing substance abuse. Law enforcement operating under different legal warrants can then ascertain whether the patient is intoxicated and take proper action (U.S. Department of Health and Human Services 1994). In situations where disclosure is required (against the patient's wishes) and may result in adverse consequences, such as the loss of a driver's license, clinicians should approach the task therapeutically, attempting to minimize damage, maximize authority, and preserve the treatment relationship when possible (Felthous 1993).

Addiction professionals frequently are involved with clients whose treatment is mandatory. This coercive aspect of care can generate conflicts between the professional's duty to honor the autonomy of the patient and to observe the constraints of adjudication, probation, or parole. Confidentiality regulations apply even to mandated clients unless disclosure is an official condition of judicial proceedings. Confidentiality protections still apply to this criminal justice consent, but there are also specialized criteria, and clinicians should obtain expert consultation on handling these cases. It is also prudent to obtain consent for disclosure that will remain in effect throughout the treatment period when criminal justice consent is not applicable. This consent should, where possible, limit disclosures to reporting on adherence and progress in treatment or danger to self or others (Brooks 2005). This approach equally satisfies the law and enables a clinician to establish an atmosphere of at least circumscribed trust, honesty, and privacy in which to do clinical work (Center for Substance Abuse Treatment 1994).

Even when consents have been obtained, the clinician should remember that he or she is first and foremost a health care professional (not a police officer!). The health professional has a positive duty to bring benefit to the patient as a priority, whereas a police officer must think about community needs and protection as a priority. It is the court's responsibility to identify positive toxicology screens and to take appropriate action; it is the provider's duty to address any substance use therapeutically. Holding the patient appropriately accountable may not only resolve the ethical dilemma but also be therapeutic. Coercion is a quality not of treatment but of criminal justice involvement, and the client has made certain choices related to substance use that in our society result in legal restrictions of the right to confidentiality and self-determination. Operating out of motives of compassion and respect for persons, clinicians can in fact utilize these very constraints for the good of the patient through reporting regular attendance and participation in treatment—conditions to be fulfilled for the patient to regain autonomy and privacy.

Perhaps the most difficult example of the conflict between beneficence toward the patient and truth telling is when the mandated client "uses" his or her limited autonomy to relapse or not adhere with recommended treatment. Yet even here, truth telling from the addiction professional may lead to short-term adverse consequences, such as incarceration, but long-term achievement of treatment goals. For some clients, external consequences, which may be experienced as coercive, may be necessary "drivers" toward motivation for recovery (Bogenschutz 2004).

Pressure from families, employers, or insurance companies is a far more pervasive and subtle form of coercion, but the same patient-centered gyroscope will help an addiction professional navigate these situations (Marlowe et al. 1996). Clinicians should acknowledge to patients and themselves the unfortunate reality that disclosing a substance use disorder may cause a patient to lose employment or health insurance. Although it is tempting to "doctor the chart" to avoid documenting substance use, the better practice is to objectively and nonjudgmentally record the substance use disorder and its relevant medical or psychosocial implications. The clinician should not embellish with extensive details that could be misused or misinterpreted, but all information necessary or valuable to patient care should be recorded. Although many providers disagree with the lack of parity for substance use treatment and government policy that funds a forensic rather than disease model of addictions, these political beliefs must not compromise accurate record keeping, which is essential for patient safety and the integrity of professional judgment (Dwyer and Shih 1998). More appropriate action on the part of the clinician is working through professional organizations and the political process to change funding mandates, organizational policies, and social attitudes that adversely affect addiction treatment. Clinicians and patients can together decide whether and what type of data to disclose to employers or insurance companies and may decide that the wisest course is to pursue self-help groups or sliding-scale treatment that protects patient privacy and livelihood.

Conclusion

Three of the top five most common reasons individuals did not receive treatment for drug or alcohol use in 2005 have an inherent ethical valence that will require substance abuse clinicians to make difficult ethical decisions, often without clear policy direction or established legal precedent. First, 38 percent of patients were not ready to stop reinforcing the neurobiological alterations of their thinking and willing. Second, 35 percent cited cost or insurance barriers, which challenges clinicians to act personally and politically to advocate on behalf of addiction treatment while respecting the law and professional ethics. Third, 24 percent cited stigma or negative opinions as the major barrier, underscoring the balancing of risks and benefits inherent in treating persons with substance use disorders (Substance Abuse and Mental Health Services Administration 2006). Despite these formidable challenges, the skill set and body of practical knowledge presented in this book can guide addiction clinicians to identify and resolve the practical moral and legal dilemmas encountered in the daily hard and good work of caring for persons with addictions.

Confidentiality and truth telling carry a special significance in the treatment of substance use disorders because of the stigma associated with addiction and the far more prominent role of the criminal justice system in addiction treatment than in other branches of health care. Federal regulations provide a higher level of protection for health information regarding substance use disorders yet also create ethical dilemmas for addiction professionals who must balance considerations of autonomy and confidentiality toward the patient with those of safeguarding the public, preventing harm, and respecting the law. Practical knowledge of the applicable law, discreet documentation, frequent consultation, and a commitment to a comprehensive view of the patient's good can help providers successfully resolve even the most troubling and complex cases.

Core Concepts

- Substance use disorders as biopsychosocial spiritual conditions require a high standard of ethical knowledge and professional skill among those caring for patients with addictions.

- Substance use disorder patients may have limited internal autonomy due to their addiction and are frequently subject to coercion from external sources, requiring the clinician to ensure that full and authentic informed patient consent is respected.

- Substance use disorders often involve illicit drugs, high-risk behaviors, and criminal conduct intersecting with the legal system, making it imperative that addiction professionals understand their professional and legal obligations and how these affect the therapeutic alliance.

- Substance use disorders are the object of powerful social stigma, and clinicians need to be aware of their own biases, which could negatively affect the therapeutic relationship.

- Substance use disorders do not have parity in funding compared to other medical conditions, leading to an immense treatment gap and the need for clinicians to act professionally for social justice.

- Substance use disorders are given higher levels of federal confidentiality protection to facilitate treatment and protect against discrimination, and clinicians need to be aware of these more rigorous standards.

Recommended Readings

Brooks, M. K. 2005. Legal aspects of confidentiality and patient information. In *Substance abuse: A comprehensive textbook,* ed. J. H. Lowinson, P. Ruiz, R. B. Millman, and J. G. Langrod, 1361–82. 4th ed. Philadelphia: Lippincott Williams & Wilkins.

Roberts, L. W., and A. R. Dyer, eds. 2004. *Concise guide to ethics in mental health care.* Washington, D.C.: American Psychiatric Publishing.

Case Examples	Core Concepts
A psychologist working in a veteran's affairs hospital is asked to evaluate Bob, a fifty-six-year-old with alcohol dependence, for a liver transplant. Bob had been abstinent for five years but recently relapsed when he learned his liver was failing. If the psychologist documents the resumed drinking, it is likely that Bob will be removed from the waiting list.	The optimal approach to disclosure of information in treatment of substance use disorders, even when mandated, is to obtain patient consent.
Rita, who works as a bus driver, seeks treatment for cocaine dependence at a local treatment center. She is a single mother supporting her three children below the age of ten. Her last two urine toxicology screens have been positive despite regular attendance at group and individual counseling, and she requests that the social worker managing her case not report her use.	A useful standard of disclosure is to release only the type and amount of information necessary to answer a specific query.
Nick, a twenty-five-year-old entering mandated treatment for amphetamine dependence and manufacturing, discloses to his addiction counselor that he killed a man several years ago during a fight over drugs. Nick and the court have each signed a consent to disclose. The counselor is unsure of her obligations.	Federal regulations provide a higher level of protection for patient confidentiality in addiction treatment.
Beth, a pediatric nurse, has achieved nearly a year of recovery working closely with an addiction therapist. As the result of severe family stresses, Beth relapses and while intoxicated calls her therapist and says she will drink herself to death. She hangs up on her therapist when he asks her to come in voluntarily. The therapist worries that if he sends the police to bring her into the emergency department for evaluation, Beth will no longer trust him and may discontinue treatment.	Truth telling and confidentiality obligations may conflict with other major ethical duties, such as nonmaleficence, autonomy, and respect for the law.
An addiction psychiatrist is caring for Tyrone, a forty-five-year-old veteran with chronic pain whose pain has been well controlled on opioids. Tyrone has been abstinent from alcohol for five years. A routine "tox screen" shows that Tyrone is positive for marijuana, which according to facility policy will mean the opioids will likely be tapered. Tyrone indicates he is using the marijuana only periodically to help him sleep.	Stigma and legal involvement heighten the importance of confidentiality in addiction treatment.

2

The Therapeutic Relationship
in Substance Abuse Treatment

JENNIFER KNAPP MANUEL, M.S.
ALYSSA A. FORCEHIMES, PH.D.

Researchers and clinicians often ask, "Which treatment intervention works best for whom?" Findings from treatment outcome studies indicate that clinician characteristics are just as important as, if not more important than, the type of intervention (Crits-Cristoph et al. 1991). According to Miller and Rollnick (2002), "The way in which one interacts with people appears to be at least as important as the specific approach or school of thought from which he or she operates." Recent research and clinical attention has focused on how to strengthen the therapeutic relationship, and a primary goal for clinicians treating patients with substance abuse problems is to establish a positive therapeutic relationship with patients early on in the treatment process, since early patient–clinician relationships predict treatment retention, adherence, and outcome (Miller and Rollnick 2002). Thus, a strong therapeutic relationship is the foundation for successful treatment. This chapter will discuss characteristics indicative of a good therapeutic relationship, as well as potential ethical conflicts related to the therapeutic relationship in the treatment of substance use disorders.

Clinician Characteristics

According to Carl Rogers (1959), three clinician characteristics are important in behavior change: empathy, genuineness, and nonpossessive warmth. Of these, empathy has received the most attention and is consistently linked to treatment outcomes. Clinician empathy has been described as the ability to actively listen to the patient and to understand the patient's perspective. Motivational interviewing (MI), an empirically supported treatment for alcohol and drug use, is based on accurate clinician empathy and reflective listening (Miller and Rollnick 2002). MI approaches the clinician–patient relationship as a collaborative effort in which the clinician seeks to support the patient's autonomy while discussing the patient's reasons and motivation to make a specific behavior change.

Research on the Therapeutic Relationship

Numerous studies indicate that a strong, empathetic therapeutic relationship between clinician and patient can improve treatment outcomes in many ways, including lower rates of drug use while the patient is in treatment and beyond. Simpson and colleagues (1997) found that a strong therapeutic relationship between the clinician and the patients attending a methadone maintenance program for opiate addiction was significantly associated with time in treatment, session attendance, and decreased opioid and cocaine use during treatment. Miller, Taylor, and West (1980) found that independent observer ratings of clinician empathy accounted for 67 percent of the variance in posttreatment patient drinking outcomes. The number of years the clinician had been working in the field was not related to observer ratings of clinician empathy nor to drinking outcomes. In a later study, Miller, Benefield, and Tonigan (1993) randomized patients to receive either directive therapy or client-centered therapy. Clinicians in the directive therapy condition were more confrontational with their patients and offered fewer listening, questioning, and restructuring responses. Results indicated that confrontational statements by the clinician predicted patient drinking such that the more the clinician confronted, the more the patient drank alcohol.

Ethical Concerns regarding the Therapeutic Relationship in Substance Abuse Treatment

The therapeutic relationship is complicated, and the nature of the relationship between a clinician and patient poses distinct ethical challenges within the treatment of substance use disorders. The patient presents for treatment seeking the expertise of the clinician, with a specific expectation of what is desired from treatment (for example, fulfilling legal obligations, achieving abstinence, harm reduction). The clinician, in accordance with principles of beneficence (benefiting the patient) and nonmaleficence (not harming the patient), has two roles in the relationship. The first role—in accordance with beneficence—is to display accurate empathy, interact genuinely, display appropriate warmth, and deliver empirically based substance use treatment interventions. The second role—in accordance with nonmaleficence—is to anticipate, self-reflect upon, monitor, and respond appropriately to ethical dilemmas that present in the context of the therapeutic relationship.

According to the American Psychological Association's Ethical Principles of Psychologists and Code of Conduct (2002), clinicians should discuss the nature of the therapeutic relationship, including the course of therapy, financial arrangements, and limits of confidentiality, with patients early in treatment. In addition, if the clinician is a resident, intern, or student, the clinician should notify patients that the case will be supervised and should give the supervisor's name. Finally, in order to avoid possible misunderstandings, the clinician should make every effort to convey the guidelines of therapy in a manner that the patient can easily comprehend.

Clinician Boundaries

An important aspect of a positive therapeutic relationship is maintaining appropriate boundaries with patients throughout the course of therapy. Examples of appropriate boundaries are starting and ending sessions on time, setting limits regarding patient contact with the clinician outside of scheduled appointments, and maintaining a professional relationship with patients at all times. Boundary violations occur when clinicians disclose personal information that is self-serving rather than beneficial to the patient, pay special attention to a particular patient, or engage in dual relationships (Nielsen 1988). Clinicians who are in recovery from alcohol or drug abuse may allow boundary violations to occur when they overidentify with their patients or allow their personal experience to interfere with the treatment of their patients.

Boundary crossings, which are often viewed as less severe boundary transgressions, differ from boundary violations in that the patient is not actively being exploited or harmed. Examples include self-disclosure on the part of the clinician in a therapy session, innocuous touching of a patient, conducting treatment sessions outside of the clinic, and starting or ending sessions late (Barnett 2007). Boundary crossings are not always inappropriate and may be utilized in order to meet the patient's needs.

Clinicians in Recovery

A number of substance use clinicians are drawn to work in the field as a result of their own recovery. According to a survey of members in the National Association of Alcoholism and Drug Abuse Counselors (NAADAC) Education and Field Research Foundation (1995), 58 percent of NAADAC counselors are in recovery from alcohol or drugs, which presents unique ethical dilemmas.

One ethical issue faced by any clinician in recovery is how much to disclose about his or her own recovery to patients. In a survey of certified counselors (Gibson and Pope 1993), 92 percent indicated that they use self-disclosure as a therapeutic technique with patients. Self-disclosure may be seen as an opportunity to bond with the patient and to demonstrate that the clinician can relate to the patient's struggles. Self-disclosure may also help the therapeutic relationship by leading to increased trust and respect due to the similarities in experience. However, the therapeutic relationship may also become more personal, less formal, and less professional (Doyle 1997). The patient may also feel comfortable asking the clinician personal questions regarding his or her recovery (Chapman 1997). It is also possible that patients may be upset to learn that their clinician is in recovery, or there may be feelings of competition between the clinician and patient (Dilts, Clark, and Harmon 1997). According to Norcross and Hill (2005), "The research suggests that therapists should disclose infrequently and, when they disclose, do so to validate reality, normalize experiences, strengthen the alliance, or offer alternative ways to think or act. . . . Therapists should generally avoid self-disclosures that are for their own needs, remove the focus from the client or blur the treatment boundaries." If clinicians choose to reveal personal information to patients, they should limit how much they disclose to patients, reflect on the reasons for the particular disclosure, and consider possible consequences.

A second ethical dilemma possibly faced by clinicians in recovery, particularly those living in small towns, is encountering patients outside of therapy. For example, clinicians may see patients at Twelve Step meetings (Doyle 1997). St. Germaine (1996) found that 47 percent of certified addiction counselors surveyed sometimes encountered their patients outside of therapy, while 21 percent encountered their patients outside of therapy frequently or daily. This poses a problem to both the clinician and the patient. To begin, if a clinician sees a patient at a Twelve Step meeting and has not disclosed to the patient that he or she is in recovery, the clinician's anonymity will be broken. It also changes the nature of the relationship in that the patient now has more information regarding the clinician's personal life. The clinician also may feel uncomfortable disclosing personal information at Twelve Step meetings in the presence of the patient. In addition, Twelve Step members often socialize after meetings. This could lead to feelings of resentment by the clinician and possibly isolate the clinician from his or her recovery network.

Clinicians in recovery may face a third type of ethical problem if they begin using alcohol or drugs again. Clinicians who return to problematic substance use may be reluctant to seek help because they are embarrassed to tell their colleagues or supervisors. In addition, they may fear losing their job or having their patients find out, which could potentially compromise the therapeutic relationship, because the patient may no longer respect the clinician and may have doubts about the clinician's effectiveness as a substance abuse provider.

Dual Relationships with Patients

Engaging in dual or multiple relationships with patients is discouraged among behavioral health providers in all areas of mental health. According to the American Psychological Association's Ethical Principles of Psychologists and Code of Conduct (2002), multiple relationships can include "a psychologist [who] is in a professional role with a person and at the same time is in another role with the same person." Professional organizations such as the American Psychological Association and the National Association of Alcoholism and Drug Abuse Counselors are very clear that counselors and psychologists should not engage in sexual behavior with current or former patients; however, other relationships, such as friendships or acquaintances in Twelve Step programs, are not clearly specified.

In a recent study, St. Germaine (1996) surveyed 858 certified alcohol and drug counselors on the ethics of posttherapy friendship. Of those surveyed, 31 percent indicated that it was ethical under rare conditions, 19 percent reported that it was ethical under some conditions, 6 percent said it was ethical under most conditions, and 4 percent indicated that becoming friends with a patient following treatment was always ethical. Moreover, 36 percent indicated that they did, in fact, become friends with a patient after therapy was terminated. The sample in St. Germaine's study consisted of both recovering (53 percent) and nonrecovering counselors, and although recovering counselors have the potential to encounter their patients in Twelve Step meetings, they did not differ from nonrecovering counselors in their responses regarding their ethical beliefs or behaviors. In a study examining certified substance abuse counselors' beliefs regarding multiple relationships, Hollander et al. (2006) found that nonrecovering individuals saw more behaviors regarding multiple relationships to be ethically concerning than recovering individuals. However, recovering counselors, in contrast to nonrecovering counselors, indicated that they would prefer to discuss issues of ethics and law in supervision (Culbreth and Borders 1998).

Forming friendships with former patients raises a number of ethical concerns. A terminated patient may want to resume a therapeutic relationship with his or her clinician but, because of the shift in their relationship from patient/clinician to friends, this would no longer be an appropriate therapeutic relationship for the patient. In addition, because of the initial patient/clinician nature of the relationship, there is an imbalance of power that is difficult to overcome in a friendship (Bovee 1998).

Duty to Warn

Tarasoff v. Board of Regents of the University of California (1974, 1976) mandates that clinicians protect individuals from the threat of serious violence by their patients. Thus, clinicians are required to act when a patient threatens an identifiable individual with violence, such as by warning the intended victim or notifying law enforcement. This mandate on clinicians to "take reasonable steps to avoid harming their clients/patients . . . and to minimize harm where it is foreseeable and avoidable" (APA 2002) conflicts with the ethical standard that "psychologists disclose confidential information without the consent of the individual only as mandated by law or where permitted by law for a valid purpose" (APA 2002). Although it is important to understand when it is appropriate and necessary to disclose, it is equally important to know when it is *not* appropriate to disclose. The two key factors are whether an intended victim is identifiable and in imminent danger.

When considering whether to breach a patient's confidentiality, it is also important to assess the likelihood that a patient will carry out a specific threat made to an individual. It is recommended that clinicians consult with other colleagues, refer to ethics codes, and consult with lawyers to determine the appropriate course of action.

Personal Value Judgments

The personal values of both the clinician and the patient influence therapy goals as well as the means by which these goals are achieved. Clinicians are often naïve in considering their own values as an ethical concern. In a survey of psychologists' adherence to the APA code of conduct, Pope and Vetter (1992) asked 679 psychologists to describe ethical dilemmas they had encountered. Of the incidents described, none concerned value conflict or conversion. Given the vital role of the interaction between clinician and patient goals in the therapeutic setting, it seems likely that these numbers reflect a lack of awareness rather than a true absence of value conflicts. Clinicians should consider gaining a better understanding of their own values through self-reflection and should have an outlet that promotes increased awareness of how values are likely to be implicitly or explicitly promoted in therapy. Some questions that would be useful to consider include the following:

- What are the clinician's goals and how do they relate to the patient's goals?
- What is considered a successful treatment?
- How will personal/theoretical values be discussed with the patient?

A clinician should respect the patient's autonomy to choose his or her own goals (APA 2002). This implies the need for clinicians to become aware of and manage their own values as they conflict with those of the patient. The needs of the patient have priority in the therapeutic relationship, and discrepant values or goals must be addressed and resolved in a respectful manner.

Scope of Practice

Recent studies indicate that between 30 percent and 60 percent of drug abusers have a concurrent (co-occurring) mental illness (Volkow 2003). If clinicians are not adept at treating mental illness, they are responsible for referring patients to another professional. Similarly, clinicians should be cautious not to overlook a medical issue or to offer suggestions that fall outside of their training. If patients inform clinicians that they are having medical problems, it is the clinician's duty to refer the patient to a physician.

Coercion

Family members or loved ones, courts, employers, public assistance programs, and school settings can coerce patients to receive substance abuse treatment. According to Miller and Miller (1998), "When voluntary consent for treatment is undermined by an element of coercion, patients lose power. Clinicians, whether they like it or not, become imbued with additional power that normally is not part of the treatment contract." When clinicians are treating a coerced patient, they have a responsibility to both the patient and the individual or system referring the patient to treatment (Miller and Miller 1998). Thus the patient may have concerns about confidentiality and be less willing to disclose.

Conclusion

Maintaining a collaborative, empathic relationship while keeping in mind ethical and legal guidelines requires a careful balance for clinicians. It is important that clinicians engage in ongoing consultations with colleagues when ethical questions arise. Table 2.1, Strategies to Maintain an Ethical Therapeutic Relationship, provides general strategies to maintain an ethical therapeutic relationship.

TABLE 2.1

Strategies to Maintain an Ethical Therapeutic Relationship

1. Review and understand ethics codes of licensing organizations.
2. Review and understand state guidelines pertaining to clinicians.
3. Consult with colleagues when ethical dilemmas arise.
4. Maintain appropriate boundaries.
5. Use caution when engaging in multiple relationships with patients.
6. Explore personal values as they relate to those of patients and address potential value conflicts.

Core Concepts

- The therapeutic relationship develops quickly and is strongly related to treatment outcomes.

- Clinicians in recovery face additional ethical dilemmas, including determining whether to disclose their own recovery status to patients and seeing patients at Twelve Step meetings.

- Clinicians have a duty to warn if there is a deliberate and imminent danger against an identifiable person.

- Clinicians must be aware of and manage their own values, especially if they conflict with those of their patients.

- Given the high rate of comorbidity between substance use and other psychiatric and medical diagnoses, clinicians must recognize and practice within their scope of expertise.

Case Examples	*Core Concepts*
Pat's patient just lost her husband and is completely distraught. She has been crying uncontrollably throughout the session. At the end of the session, the therapist touches the patient's hand in a sympathetic gesture.	Maintaining appropriate boundaries
John, a certified drug and alcohol counselor, has attended Alcoholics Anonymous for many years and considers the other members to be close friends and an integral part of his recovery. One day, John sees one of his patients at the meeting.	Dual relationships
Sam has been treating Alice for alcohol dependence. One day Alice tells Sam that she lessens the frustration of the rush hour commute by drinking three beers while driving and that she feels fine to drive because she has a high tolerance for alcohol.	Duty to warn
Dr. Jones has been completely sober for twenty years and credits this to working the Steps of AA and associating with nonusing individuals. An alcoholic patient asks Dr. Jones for help to learn how to effectively control alcohol consumption.	Personal values of the clinician

Recommended Readings

AA guidelines for AA members employed in the alcoholism field. http://www.alcoholics-anonymous.org/en_pdfs/mg-10_foraamembers.pdf.

Bovee, C. N. 1998. Multiple role relationships and conflicts of interest. In *Ethics in psychology,* ed. G. P. Koocher and P. Keith-Spiegel. New York: Oxford University Press.

Doyle, K. 1997. Substance abuse counselors in recovery: Implications for the ethical issue of dual relationships. *Journal of Counseling and Development* 5:428-32.

The Ethics of Harm Reduction

WILLIAM R. MILLER, PH.D.

The term "harm reduction" describes a public health approach intended to reduce risks and adverse consequences of behavioral choices. It is generally seen as an alternative to "zero tolerance" or total prohibition of certain behaviors or lifestyles. It acknowledges that people always have engaged and always will engage in risky behaviors (e.g., drug use, prostitution), despite potential consequences and efforts to dissuade them. The central argument is that given this reality, efforts should be made to prevent, or at least diminish, resulting harm to the individual and to society.

This chapter will describe the arguments for and against harm reduction and will detail this approach particularly as it relates to the use of alcohol. A framework for approaching the ethical considerations for harm reduction will also be given—one that addresses acceptability, feasibility, potential for harm, and potential for benefit.

Harm Reduction

The prevention and reduction of harm are certainly central ethical concerns in both research and intervention. Beneficence and its correlate of nonmaleficence (first, do no harm) are ethical cornerstones of clinical practice. In human research, institutional review boards have a responsibility to prevent or minimize harm to participants and to weigh potential risks against anticipated benefits.

Should clinicians treating people with substance use disorders, then, practice with a goal of harm reduction? On the surface it sounds self-evident, because reducing harm and alleviating associated suffering is a core value of the helping professions. The issues are complex, however, and heated debate has arisen regarding harm reduction in addiction treatment, to the extent that the National Institute on Drug Abuse has been prohibited from even using this term in its publications. The impassioned disagreements have not been about a general aim of reducing harm to patients and those around them, for on that issue virtually all would agree. Rather, the controversy has arisen around specific goals or practices that have come to be associated with this term.

Critics of harm reduction are usually concerned that such strategies appear to condone or even encourage the risky behavior, which may also be regarded as inherently immoral. The usual alternative to a harm reduction philosophy is one that promotes only total abstinence, with the behavior's associated risks and harms regarded as a natural deterrent. See Table 3.1, Ethical Questions with Regard to Harm Reduction, for a list of ethical questions clinicians may face in seeking to reduce harm to patients.

Controlled Drinking: A Prototypic Example

Arguably the first, and certainly one of the more impassioned, harm reduction controversies in modern substance abuse treatment arose in relation to therapeutic goals for people with alcohol problems: Should people be permitted to pursue a goal of moderation rather than abstinence from alcohol? This historic debate provides a prototype for pondering some of the ethical complexities of harm reduction.

The controversy began in the 1960s and 1970s with the appearance of research reports that a proportion of people who had been treated for alcoholism were found at follow-up to be drinking moderately and without apparent problems (Armor, Polich, and Stambul 1978; Davies 1962). These peer-reviewed reports in scientific journals stimulated accusations that the studies

TABLE 3.1

Ethical Questions with Regard to Harm Reduction

Is it ethical for clinicians to

1 • exchange clean syringes for used ones in order to reduce the spread of infection?

2 • help smokers or drinkers reduce their use when they seem unable or unwilling to quit?

3 • encourage drug users who are unwilling to abstain to use in less hazardous ways, such as switching from injection to lower-risk routes of administration, or to step down to less dangerous drugs?

4 • provide heroin users with life-saving naloxone injection kits to use if they should witness an opioid overdose?

5 • help drinkers plan alternatives to driving when they are intoxicated?

6 • prescribe and provide opiates through clinics for people who are addicted to heroin and unwilling to abstain?

were flawed or fraudulent, or at least that their findings should not have been presented because they could cause abstinent alcoholics to relapse (Tiebout et al. 1963). Though no such harm was documented, the fear arose from a prevalent belief at the time that alcoholics are constitutionally incapable of drinking moderately and thereby qualitatively different from nonalcoholics, who can drink with impunity. In essence, the argument was that moderate drinking by alcoholics is impossible, and therefore the reports must be erroneous.

Much has changed in the ensuing decades. A person's percentage of days abstinent has become a focal outcome measure in clinical trials, and moderate, problem-free drinking is a routinely reported phenomenon (Anton et al. 2006; Project MATCH Research Group 1997). Federally published guidelines are available for safe drinking (National Institute on Alcohol Abuse and Alcoholism 1996) and for helping people to decide between abstinence and moderate drinking goals (Miller, Zweben et al.

1992). Alcohol use disorders are recognized to be distributed along a continuum rather than dichotomous (Institute of Medicine 1990), and the National Institute on Alcohol Abuse and Alcoholism (NIAAA 2005) now encourages brief intervention to help heavy drinkers reduce their use to a safe level.

Embedded in this controversy is an assumption that such decisions (between abstinence and moderation) should not be left to patients themselves, lest they make the wrong choice. As recently as the Project MATCH study (Project MATCH Research Group 1993), clinicians were required by NIAAA to specify that the only goal of treatment was total abstinence, regardless of the patient's preference. Such dictating of the goal of treatment regardless of a patient's wishes is rather unusual in health care. That it was argued to be ethically necessary for providers to do so implies a kind of *in loco parentis* for people incompetent to make their own choices. In truth, it is virtually impossible for any person to remove another's self-determination (Deci and Ryan 1985; Frankl 1963). Attempts to restrict freedom of choice may even backfire, increasing a person's resolution to persist in the restricted action—a social psychological phenomenon known as reactance (Brehm and Brehm 1981).

Ethical Considerations in Harm Reduction

What is more often asserted now in critiques of harm reduction is that a provider should oppose rather than collude with a patient's misguided choices. In this case, an important aspect of ethical analysis is a definition of what constitutes a misguided choice. Any of at least three criteria seem to apply here: that the choice is (1) likely to result in harm to the person; (2) likely to result in harm to others; or (3) inherently wrong in relation to an absolute moral standard.

The first of these three conditions involves a judgment about the relative likelihood of benefit versus harm. Is the choice that the person is making analogous to Russian roulette? If so, what are the provider's ethical responsibilities? At the very least, it is incumbent upon the clinician to ensure that the person understands the consequences of his or her choices. The argument was made, for example, that because moderate, problem-free drinking is impossible or at best unlikely for alcoholics to achieve, they should be told to abstain and should not be "enabled" to pursue a goal of moderation. The relative likelihood of success with abstinence or moderation, however, varies with the severity of problems and dependence. Longitudinal research found that people with lower levels of severity were actually more likely to achieve stable moderation than to abstain. As severity increased, however, the relative probability of successful moderation decreased, reaching zero at the highest levels of dependence (Miller, Leckman et al. 1992).

The second consideration also involves a judgment about relative benefit versus harm that may occur, in this case to others. An example here is a pregnant drinker, whose use of alcohol incurs the risk of lifelong harm to the unborn child. Another is a drinking driver who endangers the lives and safety of others. Legislation determines the lengths to which society may go in restraining such individuals from putting others at risk, and various methods can be used to reduce the risk of harm to others.

These first two considerations are scientifically answerable questions. What is the actual probability that a particular practice will result in benefit or harm to self or others? In contrast, the third consideration involves a moral judgment about the inherent rightness or wrongness of the practice itself, or of its outcomes.

Several years ago I received a telephone call from a White House staffer who indicated that I had been nominated to serve on the National Advisory Council on Drug Abuse, and that he first had to vet me "to determine whether I held any views that might be embarrassing to the current president of the United States." My first two answers met with the White House staffer's approval, but his next question asked whether I supported needle exchange. I indicated that in my view, research clearly shows that needle exchange reduces the spread of HIV and other infections, and that I favored it. The staffer replied, "Now you're two for three. The President opposes needle exchange on moral grounds, regardless of the outcome" (Mooney 2005). That is, the practice of exchanging clean syringes for used ones was judged morally unacceptable in itself, and the relative balance of resulting benefit or harm that it could produce was irrelevant.

A further, sometimes unspoken, issue is whether the reduction of harm is itself a worthy goal. Many of the more controversial harm reduction practices are measures explicitly intended to protect the health of people despite their risky practices. Opposition to such measures could be predicated not on the inherent unacceptability of the protective measure itself, but on the belief that such people ought not be protected from the consequences of their own actions—that adverse consequences are proper punishment for substance abuse and that the harm is deserved or even therapeutic. This perspective is focused on consequences suffered by the individual. Fewer would argue that family members or innocent others deserve to suffer the adverse consequences of a drug user's actions.

This suggests a sequence of ethical questions that can be pondered when considering the potential of a particular practice to reduce harm. First is the moral question of whether harm ought to be prevented or reduced at all. In situations where punishment is prescribed by law for a person's action, the harm attendant to punishment is intentional and regarded as justified. Harm reduction practices, however, typically address what might be regarded as natural consequences of risky behavior, such as infection, overdose, or unwanted pregnancy. Should the user and others be protected from these consequences? Allowing people to suffer the nonlethal natural consequences of their substance use is one common strategy in motivating them to seek treatment (Meyers and Wolfe 2004). Whether harm, and which harm, ought to be prevented is a moral judgment, and not one that is answerable by science.

If preventing or reducing harm is generally warranted, ethical questions then focus on the appropriateness of particular practices for doing so. Some pertinent ethical questions about a specific harm reduction practice are listed in Table 3.2, Ethical Questions about a Specific Harm Reduction Practice.

TABLE 3.2

Ethical Questions about a Specific Harm Reduction Practice

1. Is the practice inherently unacceptable regardless of its consequences?
2. Is the practice possible or feasible?
3. How likely is the practice itself to cause harm that would not otherwise occur?
4. How likely is the practice to actually prevent or reduce harm or yield other benefits?

The first of these is a moral consideration, but the remaining three can be informed by scientific evidence, if available, and involve a judgment of relative potential risks and benefits.

A Practical Example

The sequence of ethical considerations can be applied in analysis of any harm reduction practice. An illustrative example is that of a person with mild to moderate alcohol dependence who wants to pursue a goal of moderate, problem-free drinking rather than abstinence, an issue on which abundant and informative data are available.

First is the general issue of whether people who "drink too much" deserve to be treated or otherwise protected from harm. Although people in most Western societies would probably answer this in the affirmative, elements of moral judgment persist. For example, treatment for substance use disorders is currently excluded from or disadvantaged in many U.S. health insurance plans.

Acceptability

Assuming a general good will in this regard and a desire to prevent or reduce harm from a patient's overdrinking, how should a clinician proceed when a heavy drinker prefers to pursue moderation rather than abstinence? Is moderate drinking in itself reasonable and acceptable? In a culture or context where any alcohol use is prohibited, the answer may be no, as with a pregnant woman, a person with liver disease, or an adolescent under the legal age for drinking. By virtue of religious belief, a Mormon or Muslim provider may be unwilling to help a patient pursue moderate drinking. Particular treatment programs may also require, as a matter of policy, that its providers only promote a goal of total abstinence.

It is not uncommon for a provider and a patient to disagree about the treatment goal. Even in a treatment program where all patients are "required" to have a goal of abstinence, personal goals vary. I encountered such a quandary in practice when a man who had been abstinent for five years came asking for help to become a moderate drinker. I strongly advised him to remain abstinent, because he had suffered significant problems when drinking, and he was healthy and functioning well with stable abstinence. "Why take the chance?" He nevertheless insisted that he was going to resume drinking with or without me, and knowing that I had developed and tested moderation-oriented treatment methods, he asked again for my help. I reluctantly agreed to a carefully monitored trial period and taught him behavioral self-control skills to manage his use of alcohol. Happily, he did establish a pattern of quite moderate drinking, which he was still maintaining without incident at our last follow-up visit eight years later.

Feasibility

A second question is whether it is possible for a person who has had problems with alcohol to maintain stable and problem-free moderation. Documentation that such outcomes occur is now beyond question, but how likely is it? The probability of stable moderation appears to depend on the severity of problems and dependence that the person has experienced. This makes it possible to provide guidelines for providers regarding the relative likelihood of stable success with moderation or abstinence (Miller and Muñoz 2005; Miller, Zweben et al. 1992). Substantial and health-relevant reductions in alcohol use have been documented in clinical trials of outpatient treatment, with follow-ups of from one to eight years (Alden 1978; Brown 1980; Hester and Delaney 1997; Lovibond and Caddy 1970; Miller and Baca 1983; Miller, Leckman et al. 1992; Pomerleau et al. 1978; Robertson et al. 1986; Sanchez-Craig 1980; Vogler, Compton, and Weissbach 1975). Thus the possibility of helping people achieve stable moderation is well documented, although the probability of success varies with patient characteristics.

Potential for Harm

Another expressed concern is that offering even the possibility of a moderation goal, in either treatment or self-help form, could cause serious adverse events for people with alcohol problems. It was hypothesized that recovery could be delayed or aborted, needlessly delaying drinkers' recognition of their need to abstain. Concern was also raised that even the public reporting of moderation outcomes could cause stable abstainers to relapse when they would not otherwise do so (Tiebout et al. 1963).

With regard to the latter concern, there were no reported epidemics or even case reports of relapse triggered by widespread news coverage of findings that some people treated for alcoholism were drinking moderately. The former hypothesis has been tested in longitudinal trials evaluating moderation-oriented treatments. In four randomized trials in which patients in alcohol treatment were assigned to abstinence or moderation goals, no significant differences in long-term outcomes were found (Graber and Miller 1988; Pomerleau et al. 1978; Rychtarik et al. 1987; Sanchez-Craig 1980). In longer-term follow-up of four clinical trials of behavioral self-control training with a moderation goal, my colleagues and I determined that 24 percent were abstaining, 15 percent were sustaining moderation without problems, and 23 percent had substantially decreased their drinking without stably achieving our standard for moderate drinking, leaving 37 percent unremitted at long-term follow-up. Among those who were totally abstinent, many indicated that the trial period of moderation had been useful in convincing them that they should abstain (Miller, Leckman et al. 1992).

Potential for Benefit

A wide variety of morbidity and mortality risks are associated with heavy drinking. Moderate drinking guidelines have been prescribed as recommended limits within which health risks are not higher than those for abstainers, and health care providers are now routinely advised by the World Health Organization and the U.S. National Institute on Alcohol Abuse and Alcoholism to encourage their patients to observe these limits for alcohol use. Brief interventions (Moyer et al. 2002), self-directed change materials (Apodaca and Miller 2003; Hester and Delaney 1997), and behavioral treatment (Hester 2003) have all been shown to significantly reduce alcohol consumption for at-risk drinkers. Furthermore, those who attempt moderation and find it difficult may thereby be persuaded that abstinence is the better or easier course (Miller and Page 1991).

In sum, it is possible to help excessive drinkers reduce their alcohol use to moderate, problem-free levels and thereby impact a major health risk factor. Parallel methods have been applied with other drugs as well (e.g., Lozano, Stephens, and Roffman 2006). The ratio of benefit to potential harm can vary significantly across different methods described as "harm reduction" and needs to be examined empirically for each specific strategy. Ideally, including such strategies within a continuum of care would in fact reduce overall risk and harm, with low probability of causing adverse consequences that would not otherwise occur, and thereby would extend benefit to people not reached by more traditional methods.

Conclusion

The general goal of minimizing harm to substance users and others is consistent with ethical standards of beneficence and nonmaleficence, although some may regard harmful consequences as deserved or therapeutic. Within this general goal, questions that can be asked about a specific practice include whether it is (1) morally acceptable, (2) feasible, (3) harmful, or (4) beneficial. The latter three questions are scientifically answerable, although moral judgment is still involved in defining what constitutes harm or benefit. This framework was used to examine the debate regarding moderation goals in alcohol treatment, as an example of ethical analysis of a harm reduction practice.

Core Concepts

- Harm reduction is a pragmatic public health approach that seeks to minimize harm resulting from risky behavior.

- Gradualism is the acceptance and encouragement of gradual steps toward reduced risk and better health.

- Zero tolerance is a strategy opposite from gradualism, in which only adherence to an absolute standard (such as total abstinence) is accepted and approved.

- Reactance is a psychological phenomenon whereby attempts to restrict freedom or choice may paradoxically strengthen the occurrence and persistence of a behavior.

- Moderation is a change goal to reduce or otherwise alter the use of a substance to a level that is unlikely to cause harm to the user or others and is sometimes called "controlled use."

Case Examples	Core Concepts
Kary is a twenty-four-year-old street sex worker who has been injecting heroin for three years and now does so daily. She is currently HIV negative but positive for hepatitis C. On visits to a public health clinic, Kary emphasizes unwillingness to stop injecting drugs, which she describes as necessary to tolerate her work and also as a normal part of her street culture. She does, however, regularly exchange used syringes for new ones through a van that visits her neighborhood daily and uses the free condoms provided. She trusts the nurses who work in the van and often asks them for medical advice.	Harm reduction through needle exchange
Matt, a twenty-seven-year-old unemployed man, is arrested for breaking a convenience store window to steal cigarettes. His preferred drugs are stimulants, and he advanced to mainlining methamphetamine two years ago. Matt is mandated by his probation officer to attend drug treatment and was referred to an agency that publicly accepts only a goal of total abstinence from all illicit drugs. At the initial evaluation, Matt states he will "stay away from drugs." The counselor's impression is that Matt is insincere and just saying what he thinks she wants to hear. The counselor presses a bit, and this opens a discussion in which Matt expresses a desire to quit using needles but mixed willingness to reduce his other drug use. "I'll have to lay off pot because it stays in your body for so long, and they'll bust me on urine tests. But I can still drink and snort coke, and they don't care about cigarettes," says Matt. "I know when I have to see my P.O., so I'll be fine. I'm just not going to quit everything right now."	Harm reduction through gradualism
Emitt has just been arrested for the second time for driving while intoxicated (DWI). He is required to complete six months of outpatient counseling. He meets diagnostic criteria for alcohol dependence, and his average alcohol consumption of six to eight drinks per day—often on the way home from work—means that he has been driving almost daily while legally intoxicated, although he rarely feels impaired. Emitt uses no other drugs, and drinking is his main shared social activity with friends. "I'm willing to cut down some, but not teetotal."	Harm reduction through moderation

Recommended Readings

Denning, P., J. Little, and A. Glickman. 2004. *Over the influence: The harm reduction guide for managing drugs and alcohol.* New York: Guilford Press.

Marlatt, G. A., ed. 2002. *Harm reduction: Pragmatic strategies for managing high-risk behaviors.* New York: Guilford Press.

Miller, W. R., and R. F. Muñoz. 2005. *Controlling your drinking: Tools to make moderation work for you.* New York: Guilford Press.

Ethical Issues in the Treatment of Persons
with Co-occurring Disorders

CHRISTIE A. CLINE, M.D., M.B.A.
KENNETH MINKOFF, M.D.

In this chapter, we focus particularly on the application of general ethical principles with regard to treating patients who suffer from one or more co-occurring disorders (concurrent substance use and mental health disorders). There are four core concepts that will guide this discussion:

1. Individuals with co-occurring disorders are an expectation in all settings, including in substance abuse treatment settings, and represent the population with poorest outcomes and highest costs, who should ethically be prioritized for care.

2. There is an emerging body of evidence to guide effective treatment approaches and interventions in any setting for individuals with co-occurring disorders.

3. This body of knowledge can be synthesized into core principles of integrated treatment that can be applied in any substance abuse or mental health program throughout the system of care.

4. These principles can be utilized to guide the design of ethical approaches for addressing the needs of individuals with co-occurring disorders in system policy, program design, and clinical practice.

Christie A. Cline, M.D., M.B.A. ▪ *Kenneth Minkoff, M.D.*

Ethical Dilemmas in Treating Patients
with Co-occurring Disorders

A young adult man walks into an outpatient mental health clinic. He looks agitated, talking loudly to himself about his landlord "throwing me out of my castle." He appears not to have showered in several days, and he looks tired and gaunt. He smells of alcohol. As he approaches the front desk to check in, he bumps into a clinician and announces, "You need to find me a place to stay before I cause some serious problems." The young man is scared because the last place he went for help told him to leave and that it was "against the rules" to show up intoxicated.

How would you respond to this young man if you were the clinician? What is the approach your clinic formally supports through policy and procedure? Would the policy and procedure emphasize that this young man is a priority "customer" of services who should be welcomed and engaged in an empathetic and hopeful relationship? In an ethical framework, in which ideals such as beneficence, respect, autonomy, and nonmaleficence are paramount, how would we organize our clinical response to support these ideals?

Overview of Co-occurring Disorders

Over the past two decades, clinicians and administrators alike have become much more aware of—and indeed inspired to action by—the very troubling plight of individuals and families with complex behavioral health concerns, including co-occurring mental health and substance use issues. We have come to understand that people with co-occurring issues are present in both substance abuse and mental health treatment settings. We now know that this population generally has poorer outcomes at higher costs in multiple domains. We also know that, epidemiologically, people with co-occurring issues are strikingly overrepresented in hospital and emergency settings and in associated systems like correctional, homeless, and child welfare services.

Further, we know that individuals in this population are more likely to be medically involved and at increased risk of death from both medical and behavioral-health–related causes, as well as from accidents and violent means (Substance Abuse and Mental Health Services Administration 2002a). In addition, we have come to understand that the prevalence of co-occurring issues is so great in any behavioral health service population that we should position ourselves clinically, programmatically, and administratively to anticipate this complexity in every setting and in every encounter.

In short, co-occurring disorders are an "expectation, not an exception" throughout the service system (U.S. Department of Health and Human Services 1999; Substance Abuse and Mental Health Services Administration 2002b). From an ethical perspective, if our goal is to create services that are responsive to the large number of complex individuals and families who need us the most, we would expect that everything that we do, at every level (system, program, and clinician practice), would be organized on the assumption that individuals with co-occurring disorders would be prioritized for care. In fact, in most settings, in both addiction and mental health treatment, exactly the opposite is the case. In most cases, these individuals and families have not only *not* been prioritized for care but also are often perceived as "misfits" who experience themselves as unwelcome in both social and health treatment settings and who find themselves frequently excluded from necessary care.

At the program level of treatment, these individuals are often experienced as if they have "dared" to have more than one disorder in programs that are designed as if everyone had one disorder only or only one disorder at a time. Clinicians in both mental health and addiction treatment programs often have to contort the patient to fit the offerings of the program or contort the program to fit the individual patient. In addition, these patients are experienced as "misfits" at the level of the skills of most clinical staff, who feel unable to respond successfully to what the patient needs. Further, because these patients do not often "fit" into any one program, they experience feelings of helplessness, hopelessness, and frustration, and are often experienced negatively, acquiring labels such as "antisocial, manipulative, borderline, med-seeking, sociopath." As a consequence of this positioning at all levels of the program, individual clinicians and individual programs (whether addiction or mental health) may not readily provide a response to individuals with complexity that would meet the ethical standards of respect, autonomy, beneficence, and nonmaleficence. Consequently, in order to begin to organize such a response in any setting, we have to begin with a significant reframing of our basic clinical approach, so that the patients who need us the most are not experienced as misfits but, rather, are experienced as individuals whom we are prioritizing for engagement in care.

In order to accomplish this challenging repositioning, we begin with the first principle of successful treatment, based on the available evidence. Comprehensive review of the literature to develop a consensus set of principles of treatment (Center for Mental Health Services 1998) indicated that all successful treatment programs for patients with co-occurring disorders welcomed and engaged patients as desirable clients, and connected with patients through relationships and programming that was empathetic, hopeful, and integrated (treating both the mental health and substance use disorder at the same time).

Expect and Welcome Patients with Co-occurring Disorders

Consequently, the first principle of ethical treatment for patients with co-occurring disorders can be stated as follows: Patients with co-occurring disorders are an expectation, and this expectation should be incorporated in a welcoming manner into all clinical contact and program design.

Any clinician's work toward developing and welcoming systems of care for patients with co-occurring disorders (Minkoff and Cline 2005) begins with the position that our ethical responsibility in substance abuse treatment settings (in fact, all settings) is to proactively welcome patients who have complex needs, who may be desperate and confused, and who may not be able to easily or effectively ask for help. Welcoming is not just being nice; it involves developing the organized framework, at both the program level and the clinical practice level, to communicate with complex individuals in such a way that they immediately feel that they are in the right place and that they made a good decision showing up to get help.

Welcoming is therefore a fundamental method of conveying respect and ensuring beneficence at the initial contact. Moreover, welcoming emphasizes that we have a proactive responsibility not to injure a patient (nonmaleficence) because of our lack of empathetic response to the reality of the co-occurring disorder. Finally, welcoming recognizes that we have to treat the patient as an autonomous "customer" who made a choice to come to see us (even if that choice was in part coerced or strongly influenced through efforts of family, friends, other health care providers, or law enforcement). We want these patients to feel that the choice they made to seek treatment was a good one. Once we begin with the principle of welcoming, we can use the other principles of treatment (see pages 64–65) to become more organized about addressing more complex ethical situations and concerns. This will be illustrated in the remaining chapter discussion and in the case examples at the end of this chapter.

As basic as "welcoming" these patients may seem in providing the framework for an ethical response to complex people, it is not easy to achieve. Preexisting values and misperceptions can interfere with clinicians' (or programs') ability to be consistently welcoming. As an example, a lack of welcoming in mental health settings often relates to a perception that individuals with substance use disorders are simply "choosing" to increase their problems through voluntary alcohol and other drug use, and that these patients should be confronted about substance use rather than empathetically engaged in care. Similarly, a lack of welcoming in addiction treatment settings may relate to a preconception that the individual is "choosing" to be noncompliant rather than being unable to participate effectively in addiction treatment because of the challenging symptoms of a co-occurring mental illness.

These misperceptions about patients are often reinforced by historical policies in addiction treatment programs that emphasize behavior control and "consequences," which in turn may reflect the historical lack of organized appreciation in such settings of the high prevalence of co-occurring mental illness and its effect on individuals attempting to work toward sobriety.

Consequences of an Unwelcome Treatment Climate

Regardless of the reason behind the lack of welcoming for patients with co-occurring disorders, the consequences of not being welcomed are often tragic. In one state system, a review of all patients who died in behavioral health care revealed that those with co-occurring disorders died at higher rates, that they frequently died of substance-related complications that had not been identified during their clinical care, and that they frequently died (of a wide range of causes) within a short time of coming into a health care setting for help. Analysis of the death reviews indicated many potential contributors to these poor outcomes for patients with co-occurring disorders, but two of the most striking indicators related to ineffective patient engagement and retention and a pervasive inability of the program to accurately recognize the co-occurring patient population, clinically and administratively.

This same scare resourced system embarked on a multiyear system change process, in which co-occurring issues were positioned as the expectation and welcoming became a priority objective for clinical and administrative change, and recognition of and services for the co-occurring patient population improved. Along with this improvement, the outcomes for the population improved, including a significant reduction in the death rate for this population (Cline and Minkoff 2002). Ethical practice literally can be a matter of life and death for these very vulnerable patients.

Effective Treatment Approaches

But what happens after we welcome and recognize the needs of patients with co-occurring disorders? What do we do next to be helpful? For many years it could be argued that insufficient information was available to provide effective treatment interventions to patients with complex needs in usual service settings. This is no longer the case. As people and families with co-occurring issues have increasingly emerged within "traditional" services, as well as in settings such as the criminal justice system, homeless shelters, child protection services, and primary health care clinics, evidence-supported clinical interventions that are effective in helping these individuals and families have accumulated. These interventions have emerged from studying the types of strategies that have been successful in formally researched "programs" for various populations of individuals with co-occurring disorders, but have been extrapolated through a variety of clinical consensus processes (e.g., Center for Mental Health Services 1998) to develop strategies for intervention that can be used in any setting, not just in special programs. These approaches begin with basic welcoming engagement in an empathetic, hopeful, and integrated relationship (Drake et al. 2003). They also include integrated screening and integrated assessment processes, stage-specific treatment interventions (Miller and Rollnick 2002; Ziedonis and Trudeau 1997; Mueser et al. 2003), strategies for contingency management for patients in care or supervision (Shaner et al. 1997), skill building for clients in substance domains regarding managing mental health issues (Daley and Moss 2002), medication education and management (Geppert and Minkoff 2003), strategies to manage trauma-related issues (Najavits 2002), and substance abuse skills training for people with severe and persistent mental illness (SPMI) (Roberts, Shaner, and Eckman 1999), and many more.

Resources for Clinicians

There are two significant core resources that organize the available information on patients with co-occurring disorders so that front-line clinicians can translate these interventions into routine practice in any treatment settings, even within the context of existing resource constraints. The first is the Center for Substance Abuse Treatment, Treatment Improvement Protocol (TIP) 42—*Substance Abuse Treatment for Individuals with Co-occurring Disorders* (Center for Substance Abuse Treatment 2005). TIP 42 is written for substance abuse treatment providers but is helpful to any clinician working in behavioral health care. The second core resource is SAMHSA's evidence-based best practice toolkit on integrated dual disorders treatment (IDDT), which describes an organized schema for a community-based approach to integrate multiple strategies, including some of those mentioned above (Substance Abuse and Mental Health Services Administration, Center for Mental Health Services, in press; Mueser et al. 2003). The IDDT toolkit was developed originally as a special program for adults who have severe mental illness and varying degrees of substance use, but is being extrapolated into various settings working with individuals who have severe mental illness (Mueser et al. 2003).

Out of the variety of research-based consensus processes (Center for Mental Health Services 1998; TIP 42; Mueser et al. 2003) mentioned above, the authors of this chapter have organized eight key research-derived and consensus-extended principles of integrated treatment (see the core concepts listed on pages 64–65) that are placed in the context of an integrated recovery philosophy and can be applied to guide clinical interventions with complex populations in any setting (Minkoff and Cline 2004).

Conclusion

Our main purpose in this chapter is to provide a framework that allows clinicians to extend the learning from the other chapters of this book to include the vast population of patients suffering from co-occurring disorders. The most important message is that ethical practice is built on a foundation of fundamental clinical values that help patients heal. In closing, we would like to return to the welcoming illustration and to leave you with a respectful adaptation of the Serenity Prayer.

The young man in the beginning of the chapter has been fortunate to walk into a clinic that emphasizes welcoming patients with co-occurring issues and has involved front-line staff and receptionists, as well as managers and supervisors, as partners in the change process. A policy and a procedure have been developed that specifically emphasize the value of welcoming, and staff have organized processes to help them build their competency in welcoming attitudes and skills.

The clinician turns to face the young man and says, calmly, "I'm so glad you came to us for help. You sound like you need something pretty important. It was wonderful that you came to ask us for help now, so that your situation does not get worse. Great job! Would you like something to eat or a cup of coffee? It will take a little while to figure out how to help you with a place to stay, so I want you to be comfortable. I'm tied up right now, but I will free myself up or find someone else quickly, because it is very important that we sit with you to understand what you want and to get you the help you need." The young man relaxes and smiles, accepting food and drink. He knows that he came to the "right door" and that there is hope of some help from a caring person.

The Serenity Prayer of Systems Change

*Please grant me the courage to change
the things I can—my own attitudes, values, knowledge
and skills, my work, my program, my part of the system;
the serenity to accept the things I cannot change,
which is everything and everybody else; and the
wisdom to know the difference, and to be in
partnership with others who are changing as well.*

63

Christie A. Cline, M.D., M.B.A. ▪ *Kenneth Minkoff, M.D.*

Core Concepts

The Eight Principles of Integrated Treatment for Patients with Co-occurring Disorders

1. Co-occurring issues are an expectation, not an exception, and must be addressed in a welcoming manner in every clinical contact.

2. Empathetic, hopeful, integrated treatment relationships are one of the most important contributors to treatment success in any setting (Drake, McHugo, and Noordsy 1993; Mueser et al. 2003).

3. Not all individuals with co-occurring issues are the same. The national consensus four-quadrant model (National Association of State Mental Health Program Directors/National Association of State Alcohol and Drug Abuse Directors 1998) can be used as a guide for understanding service responsibility for varied populations of people with co-occurring issues based on the level of severity in both domains.

4. Case management and adequate support must be balanced with expectation, consequences, and positive contingent learning for each person at any point in time in any setting.

5. When mental health and substance use disorders coexist, each disorder is considered primary, and each needs specific and concurrent attention—integrated dual (or multiple) primary issue-specific treatment.

6. Both mental health and substance use disorders can be approached using the philosophical framework of a "disease and recovery model" (Minkoff 1991), and treatment must be matched to phases of recovery and stages of change for each problem (Prochaska, DiClemente, and Norcross 1992; McHugo et al. 1995; Drake et al. 2001).

7. There is no single correct intervention for individuals with co-occurring disorders; for each person, interventions and

program matching must be individualized according to the above principles.

8. Clinical outcomes for individuals and families with co-occurring issues must also be individualized according to the principles and must be supportive of the small bits of progress people make day by day in service of their own recovery.

The case examples listed at the end of this chapter offer a few of the many possible examples of the application of the principles to support effective treatment and ethical decision making.

These principles can be used to organize not only clinical treatment, but also strategies for addressing challenging situations in an ethical manner. For example, the correct response to a patient who presents in crisis (such as the young male patient in the opening vignette) is to apply the principle of welcoming. In order for an addiction treatment clinician to convey respect and beneficence to a patient with co-occurring disorders (especially when the clinician does not have expertise in treating mental health disorders), the clinician must not only be welcoming, but also be able to empathize with the patient's experience of having multiple disorders, be able to provide hope that the patient can be successful in receiving help for both disorders, and help the patient address both disorders as primary problems to be treated concurrently as part of an integrated treatment program. In order to better explain the connection between the integrated treatment principles, the ethical principles, and specific program and clinical strategies, specific clinical examples are detailed in the case examples.

Recommended Readings

Minkoff, K., and C. Cline. 2005. Scope of practice guidelines for addiction counselors treating the dually diagnosed. *Counselor* 4:24–27.

White, W., et al. 2005. It's time to stop kicking people out of addiction treatment. *Counselor* 6:1–12.

Case Examples	Core Concepts
Pamela, a fifty-six-year-old woman, enters into residential addiction treatment for alcoholism. Pamela also has a history of physical and sexual trauma and recurrent episodes of depression with suicidal ideation. The addiction treatment team encourages Pamela to talk about her experiences dealing with trauma and depression. The addiction treatment team also works with Pamela to encourage her compliance with the recent clinical treatment recommendations she has received for her mental health issues while incorporating attention to Pamela's mental health recovery as a part of her residential treatment programming.	Nonmaleficence Multiple primary diagnoses
Dietrick, a thirty-five-year-old man, has very poor coping skills as a result of his extensive trauma history and borderline personality disorder and begins to have extremely disruptive emotional outbursts when his needs are not immediately responded to while in an addiction treatment program. Even though Dietrick's outbursts are disruptive and "against the rules," he is not punished or discharged. Rather he is respectfully offered a choice. He is told supportively that the treatment team understands he is having this difficulty in part because of his emotional issues related to the trauma and that the program could be helpful if he wants to work with his team on developing more effective coping skills. However, if Dietrick is not ready or willing to work on better coping strategies, the disruptive outbursts will make it difficult for him and others to benefit from being in the program and he will be asked to leave. The option of outpatient services is offered as well as connection to community-based recovery support services. Regardless of Dietrick's decision, he is acknowledged for taking the steps he has taken and is offered the opportunity to return at some point if he feels ready to do this kind of work to support his recovery. Given the choice, he decides to stay and take advantage of the full support of the team to help him with all his issues.	Autonomy Balancing how much we do for people and where we empathetically detach to support learning and growth Using a phase of recovery and stage of change framework

5

Cultural and Spiritual Dimensions
of Addiction Treatment

KAMILLA L. VENNER, PH.D.

MICHAEL P. BOGENSCHUTZ, M.D.

Many of us enter the helping professions because of a strong interest in human behavior and a desire to help others with psychological difficulties. As a result of the growth of racial and ethnic minorities in the United States, the population we wish to assist is becoming more multicultural and diverse. Even well-meaning practitioners have been at a loss when faced with clients from backgrounds and cultures different from their own. The American Psychological Association's ethical guidelines (1993, 2003) state that psychologists should be multiculturally competent and know their limitations in serving diverse clients. The American Psychiatric Association's *Principles of Medical Ethics with Annotations Especially Applicable to Psychiatry* (2006) states only that "a psychiatrist should not be a party to any type of policy that excludes, segregates, or demeans the dignity of any patient because of ethnic origin, race, sex, creed, age, socioeconomic status, or sexual orientation." In this chapter, we address ethical issues in addiction treatment for practitioners working with clients from various cultures, including a special emphasis on spiritual considerations. In addition, we offer recommendations for culturally competent practice and present case examples to help illustrate these ethical principles.

Definition of Culture

In this chapter, we use "culture" in the broadest terms. Often people limit the word to reference the four predominant ethnic minority groups in the United States: African Americans, Native Americans, Hispanics or Latinos, and Asian Americans. In terms of ethical guidelines, culture has historically included ten dimensions: age, gender, race, ethnicity, national origin, religion, sexual orientation, disabilities, language, and socioeconomic status. For the purposes of this chapter, we use the term "culture" to refer to these ten dimensions with a focus on understanding the various worldviews and belief systems about illness and healing, including those of our own professions.

Ethics in Relation to Culture

Within the field of ethics, there lies a continuum of philosophies from the belief that ethical principles are universal and independent of culture to the view that ethical principles vary across cultures and contexts (Harper 2006). In the middle lies the moderate view, sometimes termed "ethical multiculturalism," which tries to accommodate both ends of the continuum, so that ethical principles may take into account cultural norms. In addition, a recent paper by Fowers and Davidov (2006) invites practitioners to adopt the view of virtue ethics. Virtue ethics asks people to aspire to our highest character development rather than simply to employ ethics in a rule-based manner. Virtue ethics asks for personal transformation and ongoing character building in order to pursue ethical multiculturalism in its highest form. In this chapter, we borrow from multiculturalism, ethical multiculturalism, and virtue ethics in treating clients from various cultures.

What Is Multicultural Competence?

For more than twenty years, Derald Wing Sue and colleagues have been promoting multicultural competence, arguing that it is a lifelong process with no endpoint. Multicultural competence incorporates three aspects: awareness, knowledge, and skills. Awareness involves identification of one's own biases and levels of openness to others, as well as awareness of other cultures. Knowledge includes both general cultural knowledge and information specific to various cultures. Skills seem to include an ability to address cultural issues and may involve empirically supported techniques, adapted techniques for specific cultures, and other techniques that may have culture-based support. Moreover, the American Psychological Association (2003) provides guidelines on multicultural practice and states that psychologists should know the boundaries of their competence and actively seek out information, consultation, or supervision or refer the client to a more qualified provider or some combination of these. Hansen and colleagues (2000) point out that simply referring all clients out is not practicable, given that there are too few psychologists from ethnic and diverse backgrounds. They recommend starting with two diverse cultural groups to expand one's multicultural competence. Interestingly, Kleinman and Benson (2006) caution against focusing too much on culture: potential unwanted side effects include the client possibly feeling singled out or stigmatized and finding the questions too intrusive. Kleinman and Benson's recommendations are summarized below.

Is Good Will Good Enough?

The good will of a practitioner is not, on its own, enough to create a multiculturally competent practice (Hansen, Pepitone-Arreola-Rockwell, and Greene 2000). Some practitioners may feel that being empathetic and holding a humanistic orientation will be sufficient when working with clients from other cultures. This stance will likely entail both errors of omission, such as not knowing what questions to ask or how to proceed (potentially acting as if all people are the same), and errors of commission, such as unintentionally conveying dominant society views of racism, prejudice, and discrimination (Bishop et al. 2002). It does not acknowledge or explore differences or sociopolitical forces, nor does it pursue social justice. Although good will is one of the necessary conditions to working effectively with people from different cultures, the ability to recognize and value differences in cultural beliefs and practices is also necessary (Fowers and Davidov 2006).

Do No Harm

Western models for working with culturally diverse clients have traditionally included three harmful models: (1) those not from the mainstream culture are inferior or pathological; (2) they are deficient in desirable genes; and (3) they are culturally deficient (Sue, Arredondo, and McDavis 1992). Most would agree that these models are paternalistic and should be avoided in keeping with the ethical standard to "do no harm."

A more recent model values differences and may be termed the multicultural model or culturally diverse model (Sue, Arredondo, and McDavis 1992). First, this model rejects the assumptions of the earlier three harmful models. Second, it recognizes that bicultural or multicultural individuals are navigating at least two cultural realms. Third, it values bicultural functioning as positive and enriching. Finally, the individual is viewed as part of larger societal forces, including racism and oppression, rather than blamed as an ethnic minority.

Another more insidious problem is that we from the dominant culture have a tendency to believe that we have the premier models of health, illness, and treatment and that we can apply our models indiscriminately with people from diverse cultures. This can send a message that we are superior and that other cultural worldviews and beliefs are inferior. Thus, we do not need to be curious about other cultural beliefs about illness and healing. It is important to balance our Western knowledge and belief systems with those of our clients. An ethical issue arises when we seek to overpower our clients and demand compliance without trying to understand their models of healing and wellness. There may be times when patient outcomes may improve if practitioners' treatment plans result from collaborating with patients based on their beliefs about illness and healing (Fadiman 1997). An ethical dilemma arises when that collaboration does not include what Westerners believe to be "best practices."

"Do no harm" also means not perpetuating erroneous negative stereotypes regarding specific cultural groups and addictions.

For example, both Native Americans and non–Native Americans alike seem to hold the erroneous belief that nearly all Native Americans drink, and many incorrectly believe that Native Americans metabolize alcohol more slowly than do non–Native Americans (May 1994). These erroneous stereotypes may be due to internalized racism and identification with the oppressor as well as media sensationalism that does not focus on the many positive outcomes, such as higher rates of abstinence among Native American men and women compared with the general U.S. norms (Spicer et al. 2003).

Beneficence and Social Justice

Beyond reeducating ourselves and our clients about cultural misinformation, ethical multiculturalism, and virtue, the principles of ethics also compel us to pursue social justice. The ethical goal of improving social justice for all involves exploring with clients how their substance use problem may be related to other sociopolitical forces, such as racism, marginalization, and powerlessness (Sue, Arredondo, and McDavis 1992). Many people have drinking problems due to the stress of accommodating or assimilating to the dominant culture. In addition, some people use substances as a way to pacify anger about the injustices that they, and their cultural group, face (Duran and Duran 1995).

Erroneous negative stereotypes of minority and marginalized groups contribute to and perpetuate social injustice. Focusing on positive substance abuse outcomes among diverse groups is one way to counteract these stereotypes. For example, as noted, there are many more abstainers among certain Native American tribes than in the general population, especially among women of most tribes (Spicer et al. 2003). In addition, Asian and black youth drink less than do their counterparts in the general U.S. population (NIAAA 2004/2005). Increasing awareness of the positive substance-related outcomes among diverse and disadvantaged groups is likely to improve both their regard for themselves and the view of those groups held by the general U.S. population.

Kamilla L. Venner, Ph.D. • Michael P. Bogenschutz, M.D.

Respect for Different Models of Health and Illness

Nonmaleficence ("do no harm") also encompasses the recognition that substance abuse assessment, diagnosis, and treatment planning are largely based on models developed by and for Euro-American males. The World Health Organization has conducted cross-cultural applicability studies and found varying drinking styles as normative among various cultures and has determined that drinking styles and norms affect the applicability of the International Classification of Diseases (ICD-10) criteria for substance dependence (Room et al. 1996). For example, because of zero tolerance for alcohol consumption in some Middle Eastern countries, a person drinking even one beer on occasion may meet those countries' cultural criteria for alcohol abuse. In contrast, due to "fiesta" drinking styles among other cultures (such as Finnish and Native American), drinking large quantities of alcohol from time to time may not be considered a problem in that context. Interestingly, a cultural norm of heavy drinking episodes or "fiesta" drinking may be an example of an unhealthy norm that people from other cultures, as well as within those cultures, would want to address. Nonetheless, many researchers believe that alcohol dependence is overdiagnosed in these cultures, given the drinking norms with long spaces of abstinence between heavy drinking episodes.

Kleinman has written extensively on how to work with clients from different cultures. Kleinman and Benson (2006) encourage an ongoing conversation, beginning with inquiring about the patient's ethnic identity and how important that may be to how he or she lives and operates. They offer seven questions to guide the discovery of the patient's understanding of the illness and treatment, or what they call the explanatory model. These questions ask what the patient names the problem; what caused the problem; the course, mechanisms, and effects of the problem; and patient fears about the problem and about treatment. As multicultural ethicists, we should respect etiological beliefs based in the spiritual realm, such as witchcraft, possession by a spirit of addiction, and disharmony (see Table 5.1, Examples of Explanatory Models of Addiction). In each explanatory model, etiological

TABLE 5.1

Examples of Explanatory Models of Addiction

Spirit possession	*Alcohol is evil and/or there is a spirit of addiction that afflicts individuals.*
Witchcraft	*Addiction is caused by magical practices of individuals with malign intent.*
Spiritual affliction	*Addiction is caused by alienation from God/Creator/Higher Power.*
Disharmony	*Addiction is caused by being out of harmony with self/others/nature/spirit world.*
Moral weakness	*Substance use or addiction is viewed as a sin.*
Character flaw	*Addicts lack impulse control, empathy, sense of responsibility, etc.*
Biological disease	*Addiction is caused by genetic factors and/or biological changes in the brain of the substance user.*
Social conditions	*Public health model: Addiction is caused by a combination of the availability and characteristics of the substance, individual factors, and environmental/social conditions.*
Developmental experience	*Addiction is caused by traumatic experience, lack of adequate attachment, and social learning.*
Intrapersonal conflict	*Psychoanalytic model: Addiction is a symptom of underlying neurosis.*

beliefs are intimately tied to treatment interventions. Just as the moral model requires punishment and the disease model necessitates treatment, the spiritual model requires spiritual intervention. Without seeking an understanding of the client's health and illness belief systems, clinicians are likely to be less effective. Rather than assuming that a lack of motivation underlies patient nonadherence with Western interventions, consider that the client may have a different explanatory model. Furthermore, nonadherence may represent other barriers related to sociopolitical forces, such as poverty, racism, and powerlessness.

Respect for Persons

Respect for persons is often used interchangeably with respect for autonomy (see Table 5.2, Ethical Principles Relating to Culture and Spirituality in Addiction Treatment). Western views of autonomy focus on individuality. Even among Western countries (such as Finland, Greece, Scotland, Germany, and Spain), views of autonomy vary by country (Leino-Kilpi et al. 2003). In many non-Western countries, such as Turkey, the smallest autonomous unit is the family. Other cultures view the individual as inseparable from the community. Our value of individual autonomy is inextricable from our emphasis on confidentiality. In 2002, Meer and VandeCreek published three case examples where consent and release of information were based on the Western autonomous view of the individual and resulted in treatment dropout and poor outcomes. The authors attributed this to lack of clarity about the cultural norms regarding who were the appropriate consenting persons, because the people who were culturally in charge of the individual felt betrayed by the therapist and client. The highlighted culture was South Asian society, where valuing individuality is diametrically opposed to the social norm of parents and elders having almost complete rights over the individual's life and choices. Meer and VandeCreek suggest discussing the opposing values with the client and asking whether and to what extent the client wants family involvement.

TABLE 5.2

**Ethical Principles Relating to Culture and
Spirituality in Addiction Treatment**

- **Respect for persons** implies respect for the cultural and spiritual beliefs, values, and experiences of persons in addiction treatment. Providers must make a good-faith effort to understand the beliefs and values of patients (which may or may not be counter to medical or psychiatric models) in order to provide care that is respectful of these perspectives.

- **Justice** requires that culturally appropriate treatment options be available to all those in need of addiction treatment. Social justice requires making efforts to ameliorate negative sociopolitical forces such as racism, poverty, and marginalization.

- **Personal responsibility and voluntarism** suggests that in order to make decisions about treatment options, patients should be provided with relevant information about all reasonable treatment options, regardless of the practitioner's attitudes toward these interventions and the explanatory models they embody. Coercion is minimized by emphasizing the patient's right to apply her or his own values to the information provided by the practitioner.

- **Therapeutic alliance** requires that cultural competence is critical to establishing an effective therapeutic relationship.

- **Beneficence/nonmaleficence** suggests that to provide the best possible care, it is necessary to incorporate cultural and spiritual dimensions into evaluation and treatment. Some beliefs and practices are objectively harmful, while others are therapeutic, so respect must be balanced with the obligation to help and prevent harm. Acting on cultural, ethnic, or religious stereotypes can have harmful consequences.

Foundational to respecting others is a deep and ongoing awareness of one's own biases, inherent in each of us. Some describe this as a natural ethnocentrism. In order to function, we are socialized into believing that our own cultural worldview is correct, which implies that it is superior to the worldviews held by others. We must become aware of our biases in order possibly to overcome them or to know when we need to refer a client to another competent provider. Respect for others requires that all treatment options be presented to the client, regardless of the practitioner's attitudes toward these interventions and the explanatory models they embody.

Realizing that cultures vary on many dimensions, we must assess differences among cultures regarding appropriate professional boundaries, multiple relationships, and conflicts of interest (for more information see the June 1, 2005, draft proposal of the Universal Declaration of Ethical Principles for Psychologists available at http://www.am.org/iupsys/ethicsdoc.html). Although most training programs are monocultural and monolingual, for ethical multiculturalists respect for biculturalism, bilingualism, and multiculturalism is necessary. However, we must beware of perpetuating erroneous negative stereotypes regarding culture and addiction.

Justice

Most everyone would agree that every individual deserves the best addiction treatment available, but it is difficult to know how to best facilitate this in our current health care system and to know which is the best treatment across cultures. It may be that best practices by Western standards (i.e., empirically supported interventions) are counter to indigenous or religious practices (i.e., culturally supported interventions). First, within our health care system, people are not provided equal access to substance abuse treatment because of lack of health insurance and lack of financial resources (i.e., inability to pay for services and lack of transportation or child care). Second, Western substance abuse treatment may be in conflict with culturally supported treatments, especially for those who are more identified with their culture as opposed to mainstream culture. Again, Kleinman's recommendations above will help guide providers of substance abuse treatment for cross-cultural clients. There are at least four possible directions for choosing treatments. One can (1) provide Western approaches in their original form, (2) provide Western approaches in a culturally adapted form, (3) provide a culturally supported intervention alone, or (4) develop a new treatment specific to a particular population (see Table 5.3, Four Interventions to Consider When Working with Patients from Various Cultures).

Each direction has pros and cons. A Western approach has the

TABLE 5.3

Four Interventions to Consider When Working with Patients from Various Cultures

Types of Interventions	Pros	Cons
Transport evidence-based treatment (EBT) as is	• Know EBT has evidence showing good outcomes in the general population	• May not be acceptable to subgroup • May be viewed as paternalistic (dominant culture knows what is best for other cultures)
Culturally adapt EBT	• Often shown to increase recruitment and engagement of other cultures, indicating higher acceptability of intervention	• Costly • Do not know how adaptations may affect patient outcomes
Use culturally supported interventions	• Likely will have high acceptability among those cultural groups (should have higher recruitment and engagement)	• Do not know the effectiveness of these interventions
Develop new interventions	• Can target unique aspects of various cultures for individual and family interventions • Likely to have higher acceptability	• Costly • Do not know the effectiveness of the resultant intervention

advantage of empirical support for efficacy but may clash with a cultural explanatory model and thus be less effective. An adapted Western approach may not have empirical support but may be more acceptable to a cultural group. The same may be the case for a culturally supported intervention or a newly developed approach.

A few substance abuse treatments have been developed specifically for a cultural group and a few have been adapted in partnership between academic and cultural community groups. José Szapocznik (2003) developed the *Brief Strategic Family Therapy for Adolescent Drug Abuse* for Cuban families, though it is applicable to other cultures that emphasize family and interpersonal relationships. Another empirically supported intervention, Project VENTURE, was designed by McClellan Hall to prevent substance abuse among Native American youth. June La Marr and Alan Marlatt (2007) integrated Native American cultural strengths with cognitive-behavioral strategies to treat and prevent Native American adolescent substance abuse in their manual *Canoe Journey, Life's Journey: A Life Skills Manual for Native Adolescents,* which can be purchased at http://www.hazelden.org/bookstore. Recently, two manuals have adapted an empirically supported substance abuse intervention for Native American clients. Kamilla Venner worked in partnership with Native Americans to develop an adapted version of motivational interviewing for use with Native American clients across tribes. This manual, *Native American Motivational Interviewing,* can be downloaded from the Center on Alcoholism, Substance Abuse, and Addictions (CASAA) free of charge at http://casaa.unm.edu/nami.html. One Sky, the American Indian/Alaska Native National Resource Center for Substance Abuse and Mental Health Services, has a manual, *Motivational Interviewing: Enhancing Motivation for Change,* that is available at http://www.oneskycenter.org/education/documents/MotivationalInterviewing1.pdf.

Biology and Ethnicity

An additional consideration is that cultural and ethnic differences may be correlated with genetic differences, which can affect predisposition to or course of substance use disorders. Knowledge of these biological differences therefore can be considered to be an element of cultural competence. Caution is in order, as the idea of genetic differences among populations has often been used to perpetuate racial stereotypes and racist agendas. However, there are genetic differences between populations that have clinical significance and should not be ignored. One well-known example is the differing frequency of alcohol dehydrogenase and aldehyde dehydrogenase genotypes in different ethnic groups. The inactive allele of aldehyde dehydrogenase is much more common in many peoples of Asian origin. Individuals with this allele have a lower risk of alcohol dependence. Another important example is the variability in genes coding for the CYP450 proteins that metabolize many therapeutic drugs as well as drugs of abuse. Gene frequencies vary markedly among different ethnic groups, and these differences can have a marked impact on rates of drug metabolism and interactions between drugs.

Spirituality and Addiction

Religion and spirituality are best conceptualized as multidimensional constructs that overlap but are conceptually distinct. Spirituality may be seen as an attribute of individuals, analogous to personality or health. Religion, on the other hand, is a social phenomenon, defined by particular boundaries, such as belief, practice, and membership. Religion is conceived as an organized system of beliefs and practices intended to mediate an individual's relationship to the transcendent and to the community. Religiousness, the extent of involvement in institutional religion, is one aspect of an individual's spirituality. Recent years have seen an increase in professional and popular interest in the relationship of spirituality and religion to health in general and in linkage of addiction, religion, and spirituality in particular (Geppert, Bogenschutz, and Miller 2007).

Kamilla L. Venner, Ph.D. • Michael P. Bogenschutz, M.D.

Why Does Spirituality Matter in Addiction Treatment?

Spiritual or religious concepts and practices have traditionally played a larger role in addiction treatment than in other areas of mental health or medicine. The spiritual model of Twelve Step programs and other religiously inspired models remain highly influential, particularly in the United States. Recent discoveries in pharmacology and psychotherapy have not diminished the salience of spiritual dimensions in the care of persons with substance use disorders.

In addition, there is considerable evidence that beliefs and behaviors, which could be characterized as spiritual or religious, have a significant influence on substance use and addiction. The most consistent findings from the voluminous literature on addiction and spirituality are (1) an inverse relationship between religiosity and substance use/abuse, (2) reduced use among those practicing meditation, and (3) protective effects of Twelve Step group involvement during recovery (Miller and Bogenschutz 2007). Treatment models based on the Twelve Step approach have demonstrated efficacy in well-controlled clinical trials, and the Twelve Step approach now ranks among the leading empirically validated forms of psychosocial treatment for addictions. Not surprisingly, atheists and agnostics are less likely than their religious counterparts to go to Twelve Step meetings. However, people who go to meetings are more likely to stay sober, regardless of their beliefs.

Ethical Principles Relating to Spirituality and Addiction Treatment

The two ethical principles most directly related to spirituality and addiction treatment are beneficence and respect for persons. Beneficence requires that we provide the most helpful treatment that we can. For the reasons delineated below, to do so it is often necessary to include spiritual/religious dimensions in the process of evaluation, treatment planning, and treatment, as well as in the therapeutic relationship itself. Respect for persons requires that the clinician make a good-faith attempt to understand the beliefs and values of the patient, in order to provide care that is consistent with, or at least respectful of, these perspectives. Other ethical principles are also involved, as discussed below and summarized in Table 5.2. The practical implications of these considerations are developed in the four recommendations that follow.

1. Ask the patient about his or her spiritual beliefs.

Traditionally, health professionals have tended not to inquire about the spiritual and religious dimensions of their clients' lives. This may be due to lack of training in the area of spirituality, lack of recognition of its importance, a sense that the topic is somehow inappropriate for discussion in a health care context, or a general bias against religion or spirituality (see the second recommendation below). Spirituality is increasingly viewed as having important implications for health and medical care. The Joint Commission now requires assessment of spirituality as a basic element of assessment in health care settings. This information is important for purposes of treatment planning because it has direct implications regarding (1) acceptability of various treatment options; (2) available resources for social, emotional, and even financial support; and (3) explanatory models of addiction and other illnesses that may affect attitudes toward treatment and recovery. More generally, asking about a person's spiritual life can help to establish an effective therapeutic relationship by demonstrating respect and making the patient feel more completely understood. As with the broader value of cultural sensitivity, sensitivity to the religious and spiritual dimensions of a patient does not require that a practitioner know everything about the patient's religion or belief system. Rather, the goal is to try to understand what is important to the particular individual. As with cultural stereotypes, false assumptions about a person's values based on his or her stated faith or background can be as harmful as ignoring spirituality altogether.

2. Avoid expressing bias for or against spirituality/religion.

Best care requires that patients be presented with appropriate treatment options, including those with and those without spiritual content. It is well known that physicians, psychologists, and other behavioral health professionals are on average much less religious than the general public. On the other hand, there are some providers, particularly in the addictions field, who adhere to a spiritual model of recovery and promote this model exclusively. Expression of either bias can be perceived as disrespectful if the practitioner appears to disparage or devalue the patient's beliefs and practices. From a practical perspective, the therapeutic alliance is likely to suffer, and this can adversely affect the treatment outcome.

3. Include spiritual/religious aspects in treatment planning.

In a broad sense, it is important to negotiate a treatment model and plan that is consistent with the patient's beliefs and values. If religion and spirituality play important roles in the patient's life, it may be important to include them explicitly in the plan for recovery. This could include Twelve Step-based treatment and meetings, a faith-based recovery program consistent with the patient's beliefs, referral to an appropriate religious or spiritual leader or authority for guidance, attendance at religious services as a recovery activity, prayer, and meditation. As with other health activities and sources of support, patients should be encouraged to look for ways that spiritual resources can support recovery. On the other hand, it is not appropriate to insist on a form of treatment that is inconsistent with a patient's beliefs and values. There are many effective forms of treatment. Again, both respect and beneficence require that the patient be involved actively in choosing the most appropriate treatment model.

4. Address countertherapeutic beliefs with factual information and respect.

Countertherapeutic beliefs present a dilemma because the beliefs should be treated with respect, but therapeutically it would be valuable for the beliefs to change. Examples are the beliefs that addiction is the result of a moral weakness or of possession by a malign spirit. These explanatory models are not consistent with available, effective models of treatment. Although it is not possible to disprove such beliefs, nor wise to try to, it is the responsibility of the clinician to present factual information regarding the dynamics of addiction and the effectiveness of treatment. Most people can tolerate some "cognitive dissonance," and explanatory models are not necessarily mutually exclusive. A person who believes she is possessed by the devil or under the influence of witchcraft may still be willing to try medications or to work on changing thoughts and behaviors that contribute to addiction. Such a person might also continue to pursue spiritual healing parallel to professional treatment and, in the absence of evidence that such ceremonies are harmful, should not be discouraged from doing so.

Core Concepts

- Culture and spirituality have significant implications for all aspects of addiction treatment, including assessment, treatment planning, treatment, and the therapeutic relationship.

- Adequate cultural competence, including awareness of one's own values and biases, is necessary to provide ethically sound addiction treatment.

- Cultural competence includes the following:

    1. knowing your own cultural worldview, biases, strengths, and weaknesses

    2. being willing to question your own training and worldview

    3. exploring the client's beliefs about addiction, its causes, and treatment/healing

    4. taking part in diverse events, celebrations, and friendships to extend your experience with diverse people from practice to experience

- In negotiating treatment plans across cultural differences, it is helpful to analyze the patient's culture in terms of elements that are helpful, neutral, and harmful with respect to recovery.

Case Examples	Core Concepts
Jon, a forty-four-year-old Euro-American male with a twenty-five-year history of schizophrenia, twenty-year history of alcohol dependence, and fifteen-year history of crack cocaine dependence, is an evangelical Christian and believes that his addictions are due to demonic oppression. Jon is disgusted with Alcoholics Anonymous (AA) because he believes it is a "watered-down" spirituality, and he says he has been asked to leave meetings because he was "preaching the word." He finds support at his church, where he has been told that he should not take psychiatric medication.	Respect for persons requires the practitioner to attempt to understand this patient's explanatory model of addiction. The practitioner should examine his or her own possible biases regarding evangelical Christian beliefs. The practitioner should look for ways to offer treatment options that are consistent with the patient's beliefs (e.g., referral to a Christian counselor/minister, framing medication effects as decreasing the power of "demons" over the patient).
Karai, a thirty-two-year-old Navajo woman, is ready for discharge after a six-week residential treatment for alcohol dependence and is considering how to stay sober once she leaves the hospital. Her husband is a recovering alcoholic who belongs to the Native American Church and wants her to join. Karai's parents are traditional Navajos, and they have arranged for her to have a week-long healing ceremony, which they believe is necessary to restore her to harmony. Karai has attended AA while in treatment, and her counselor is strongly encouraging her to continue AA after discharge. The psychiatrist has started Karai on naltrexone, which she plans to discontinue as soon as she leaves the hospital.	Assess the client's explanatory model and acceptability of various treatment models. Assess conflict between individual and family preferences, and explore family therapy options. Attempt to maximize family support for the patient's efforts toward sobriety.

Case Examples	Core Concepts
Luis, a forty-three-year-old Hispanic male, engages in time-limited cognitive-behavioral therapy (CBT) for amphetamine dependence. During therapy, Luis states that he feels as if there is a spirit of drugs that is tempting him to use and feels afraid. There is no module in the CBT manual to address this etiological belief of drug problems. The therapist asks Luis what he can do about this spiritual affliction. Luis responds that he can pray.	Clarify whether the client's belief is consistent with his belief system or could be a manifestation of psychosis. Encourage the client to use CBT tools within his own belief system (e.g., using distraction as well as prayer to deal with the "spirit of drugs").
Atian, a Native American, begins therapy with a Native American therapist. The therapist asks Atian for matches and then engages in a ritualistic smudging ceremony by burning cedar and sage. He then offers the smoking plants to Atian, so he can purify himself and send his prayers to the Creator. Atian looks confused, waves the smoke toward himself, and then says he does not practice those traditions.	The therapist should attempt to understand the client's belief system and sense of cultural identity rather than make assumptions based on stereotypes or shared heritage.
Benjamin, a Christian Scientist, does not want pharmacological treatment like disulfiram, naltrexone, or buprenorphine.	The physician should carefully explain the risks and benefits of pharmacologic treatment and should present other available nonpharmacological options.
Tyler, an "aging" forty-four-year-old white homosexual male, is Christian and reports guilt about his methamphetamine use in bathhouses to improve his sexual experience and performance.	The counselor should examine his or her own potential biases toward Christian beliefs and sexual orientation. The counselor should facilitate the client's exploration of ambivalence regarding drug use and sexual behavior.

6

Forensic Issues in the Treatment of Addictions

JOSEPH B. LAYDE, M.D., J.D.

Individuals who misuse substances present addiction treatment and other health care practitioners with a broad array of special legal and ethical issues related to coerced treatment for addictions and societal concerns about alcohol and drug dependency. Clinicians treating patients with substance use disorders may become involved in any number of clinical situations in which the legal ramifications of their work are important.

This chapter will overview civil and criminal law issues of special importance in the treatment of people living with addictions: court orders for the treatment of addiction, civil competency to make personal and financial decisions, disability from alcohol and drug dependence, confidentiality and the duty to protect the public from the actions of addicted individuals, workplace drug testing, competency of individuals who abuse substances to stand trial in criminal cases, insanity defenses in addicted patients, and the relationship of specific intent in criminal cases to substance abuse. The chapter will conclude by discussing malpractice issues encountered by clinicians treating patients with substance use disorders.

Court Orders for the Treatment of Addiction

The societal responses to the problems of alcoholism and drug dependence vary across the United States. Some jurisdictions permit the civil commitment of individuals who suffer from alcohol or drug addiction and who are dangerous to themselves or others on the basis of the addiction. Depending on state or provincial statute, the mechanisms for arranging for involuntary treatment of addicted people may differ from those used for treatment of mental illness. For example, adults with drug dependency in Wisconsin may be confined for treatment if they are dangerous to themselves or others, as defined under the same statute that applies to people with mental illness (Wis. Statutes, Sec. 51.20, 2007). The civil commitment of adults with alcoholism in Wisconsin, on the other hand, is handled under a different section of the law. Although alcoholics who are dangerous to themselves or others may receive involuntary inpatient treatment for alcoholism in Wisconsin (Wis. Statutes, Sec. 51.45, 2007), the treatment provided in some counties is generally only for an emergency period of danger due to intoxication. In a move indicative of societal concern over the effects of addiction on teenagers, Wisconsin parents have recently received more authority to place their minor children (under eighteen years of age) with substance abuse problems (whether due to alcohol or other drugs) into inpatient treatment (Wis. Statutes, Sec. 51.13, 2007).

Some other jurisdictions have very different legal schemes for treating chemically dependent patients. New Mexico, for example, does not permit long-term commitment for inpatient treatment of substance dependence, but instead permits "protective custody" of individuals incapacitated by alcohol or drugs and encourages voluntary treatment of individuals who seek help (N.M. Statutes, Sec. 43-2-8, 2006). An interesting new approach to encouraging treatment is being tried in New Mexico, where individuals who receive emergency help for drug overdoses are promised immunity from criminal prosecution for the possession of drugs found during the emergency response to the overdose (N.M. Senate Bill 200, signed into law April 3, 2007). This same statute also protects the individual's friends or family from criminal prosecution for drugs found during the emergency response overdose call. Given the geographical variation in laws on substance abuse treatment, it is important that clinicians become familiar with the procedures used in their area to encourage treatment for alcoholism and drug dependence.

The question of the ethics of involuntary treatment for voluntary intoxication with alcohol or other drugs is a thorny one. Advocates of coerced treatment argue that addicted people are in fact unable to control their use of substances and that a paternalistic approach to getting them into treatment is necessary because of the nature of addiction itself. Opponents argue that society has no business telling decisional people (adults and, arguably, older adolescents) that they must receive treatment to limit their intake of substances and must be confined for a portion of that treatment. The variety of practices for forcing addicted patients into treatment seen in different North American jurisdictions reflects conflicted societal attitudes to involuntary treatment for addiction. The twenty-first century will doubtless see a continued evolution of those attitudes.

In addition to the mechanism of civil commitment, there is another important way in which the legal system coerces people into treatment of substance-related disorders: courts will often mandate addiction treatment by requiring individuals who are involved with the criminal justice system to get treated for substance dependence as an alternative to incarceration. Clinicians may be reluctant to accept such patients into treatment, because they may be skeptical of the patients' motivation to stop using alcohol and drugs. Judges and probation agents, however, see addiction treatment with close monitoring as a real chance for some people to avoid a lifetime of incarcerations for drug-related offenses (Hardy, Patel, and Paull 2000).

Because practices in civil commitment and other court-ordered treatment vary widely among jurisdictions, it is important for addiction treatment professionals to learn the statutes and actual practices applicable in the localities where they practice.

Civil Competency to Make Personal
and Financial Decisions

Substance abuse treatment professionals are sometimes called upon to give opinions on the ability of their patients to make rational and safe decisions about how to care for themselves and their finances. In the case of pregnant women, these decisions include not exposing their fetuses to alcohol and drugs. An individual's lack of competency is a judicial determination that the person is unable to make a rational decision on a particular issue, such as the need for medical care or how to enter into a valid contract. If a professional is called to testify in a judicial proceeding on a patient's competency, it is important to know what specific competency is being questioned—for example, to consent to medical procedures or to handle finances (Gendel 2004). A guardian may be appointed if the patient is unable to make decisions on self-care, and a guardian of the estate may be appointed solely to handle a spendthrift patient's finances.

Pregnant women who expose their fetuses to dangerous levels of alcohol or other drugs have sometimes been prosecuted as criminals (Committee on Alcoholism and Addictions, Group for the Advancement of Psychiatry, 1998:149-50; Gendel 2004). More recently, there has been a movement to permit the preventive detention of pregnant women who abuse alcohol and drugs to keep them from harming their fetuses by drinking or using drugs on the theory that they cannot make good decisions to protect their soon-to-be-born babies. In Wisconsin (Wis. Statutes, Sec. 48.193, 2007) and some other states, courts may commit pregnant women who have a history of alcohol or drug dependence to inpatient addiction treatment for as long as the duration of their pregnancies (Dailard and Nash 2000). Iowa, Minnesota, and Vermont require health care workers to test some pregnant women or newborns for prenatal drug exposure (Dailard and Nash 2000). Increasing public awareness of the potential catastrophic consequences of prenatal exposure to teratogenic substances like alcohol has led society in recent years to be much stricter in protecting fetuses from the actions of their substance-dependent mothers.

Disability from Alcoholism and Drug Dependence

Clinicians are often asked to provide opinions about the degree of impairment of their substance-dependent patients who are seeking disability benefits. Private disability insurance may permit addicted individuals to receive such benefits for active addiction, but the U.S. government in the 1980s and 1990s abolished substance abuse disorders in the absence of other psychiatric or medical disorders as a cause of disabling impairment for the purposes of Social Security Disability Insurance (SSDI), Supplemental Security Income (SSI), and Veterans Affairs (VA) disability benefits (Gendel 2004).

The Americans with Disabilities Act (ADA) of 1990 offers addicted persons protection against workplace discrimination on the basis of their addictive disorders, but it treats alcoholism differently from dependence on illegal drugs, in that those addicted to illegal drugs are protected under ADA only if they are in treatment or have completed treatment for their addiction and are not currently abusing illegal drugs. The ADA requires that individuals addicted to controlled substances be under the care of a licensed health care professional to receive ADA protection. The ADA does not protect addicted people who are a danger to the safety of others (Gendel 2004).

Workplace Drug Testing

Many employers routinely screen new and current employees for drug use; urine drug screens are most commonly used. The U.S. government tests many of its own employees and requires testing of transportation industry workers. Private sector employers frequently follow federal guidelines for testing, looking for the presence of active drugs or metabolites in five groups: marijuana, cocaine, morphine or codeine, amphetamines, and phencyclidine (PCP) (Sgan and Hanzlick 2003; McKnight and Wheat 1995).

Most of those substances are excreted quickly from the body, but phencyclidine can appear in urine almost a week after use, and a marijuana metabolite can appear in urine almost a week after a single use and almost a month after the cessation of ongoing use (Osterloh and Becker 1990). Some private employers test for other drugs, such as benzodiazepines and barbiturates (Sgan and Hanzlick 2003).

Employers often hire physicians as medical review officers to interpret the results of drug testing and to determine if substances found during testing are legitimately used by the person tested (Sgan and Hanzlick 2003). Employees found to be abusing substances can be referred to an Employee Assistance Program (EAP) for assistance in finding appropriate treatment.

Confidentiality and the Duty to Protect the Public from the Dangerous Actions of Addicted Individuals

In addiction treatment, the need for confidentiality in the clinician–patient relationship is particularly clear. Many patients are embarrassed that they are dependent on substances, and often the assurance that they can receive confidential treatment allows them to seek treatment. The U.S. government recognizes the sensitivity of addiction treatment; a federal rule (42 CFR, part 2) provides protection for the confidentiality of patients suffering from or seeking evaluation for substance-related problems in federally assisted alcohol or drug treatment programs. Of course, state law, federal HIPAA regulations, and the principles of medical ethics also protect patients' confidentiality, as they would under any other circumstances in the United States.

A patient who wishes to have information about addiction treatment be part of a court proceeding, for instance, as part of a custody dispute, may authorize the release of treatment records to his or her attorney. A patient's attorney may also subpoena a treating clinician to testify in court about the patient's condition. Clinicians must be prepared to honor such demands, because the right to the confidentiality of a patient's health care information belongs to the patient, who may waive it at any time.

Occasionally, circumstances may arise that require the disclosure of what would otherwise be confidential medical records of patients in addiction treatment. Three such circumstances include the discovery of abuse of a minor in substance abuse treatment, a crime committed on the premises of a treatment facility, and a court order mandating record release (Gendel 2004).

The duty to protect a third party from reasonably foreseeable dangerous acts may require a breach of the confidentiality of a patient with a substance-related disorder. However, in order to follow the provisions of 42 CFR, part 2, a clinician warning an intended victim or the police should not reveal the specific fact that the patient involved suffers from a substance-related disorder (Gendel 2004).

Competency of Substance-abusing Individuals to Stand Trial in Criminal Cases

Individuals charged with crimes are competent to stand trial if they possess the ability to rationally and factually understand the legal proceedings they face and to rationally assist their counsel in their defense. Temporary intoxication is unlikely to be grounds for a defendant being adjudged incompetent to stand trial. For example, if a defendant who is out on bail shows up drunk at his or her trial, the judge is likely to simply postpone the matter until the defendant is clearheaded—and is likely to give the defendant a jail cell in which to sober up.

Some addicted individuals, however, develop long-lasting toxic psychoses or organic brain syndromes, such as Korsakoff's dementia, which may have a serious impact on their ability to competently stand trial for criminal offenses (Gendel 2004). A criminal defendant with a cocaine-induced psychotic disorder with hallucinations and delusions may be unable to concentrate adequately in a courtroom to assist his attorney in his defense and hence may be incompetent to stand trial; commitment for treatment with atypical antipsychotics may allow the defendant to regain his competency to stand trial within a short period. A criminal defendant with a history of alcoholism who develops Korsakoff's dementia, on the other hand, may be unable to remember essential facts about her legal proceedings and may as a result be incompetent to stand trial; treatment is unlikely to change such a defendant's mental state much, and she may never be competent to stand trial. In such cases, a judge may order the suspension of criminal charges against the defendant and may institute guardianship proceedings, which can result in the demented patient being placed in a nursing home.

Insanity Defenses in Addicted Patients

Society has never held voluntary intoxication to be a valid excuse for irresponsible or illegal actions. However, as is the case with competency to stand trial, some long-lasting substance-related psychoses and organic brain syndromes may affect behavior in such a way as to occasionally be considered exculpatory for defendants accused of a crime (Gendel 2004).

Even if a mental disorder such as a psychosis or dementia has the potential to cause a person to act contrary to the law, it will only constitute a valid insanity defense in a jurisdiction that recognizes the insanity defense to begin with, and then only if a criminal defendant acted in a way that meets a jurisdiction's insanity defense.

Most states and the U.S. government use some variation of the M'Naughten Test, which is purely a cognitive test for insanity. The M'Naughten Test requires that, as a result of mental disease or defect, a defendant either did not know the nature and quality of his criminal act or, if he knew it, did not know that what he was doing was wrong. Some states use a variety of the American Law Institute Test for insanity, requiring that, as a result of mental disease or defect, a defendant either did not know the wrongfulness of her action or was unable to conform her actions to the requirements of the law—a test with a cognitive and a volitional prong.

The Relationship of Specific Intent in Criminal Cases to Substance Abuse

Although voluntary intoxication does not qualify a defendant for an insanity defense, some crimes require, as one of the elements of the offense, that a defendant have a particular mental state at the time of the crime (Mack and Lightdale 2006). In some jurisdictions, for example, a finding of first-degree intentional homicide requires that the defendant actually intended to kill the person. Intoxication with alcohol or other substances may so impair a person's faculties as to make him unable to intend to kill a person. Expert testimony from a psychiatrist may be admitted at a trial to indicate that a defendant was so drunk that he could not have intended to kill the stranger he stabbed during a bar fight. In such a case, the defendant would likely be found guilty of a lesser offense, such as manslaughter.

Malpractice in Addiction Treatment

Addiction treatment professionals face the same risks as other mental health clinicians of malpractice claims for negligent misdiagnosis and treatment of their patients. Patients with addiction problems have relatively high rates of suicide, and suicide is a frequent cause of allegations of malpractice by all mental health professionals.

Malpractice claims against nonphysician professionals are likely to relate to allegations of a breach of confidentiality, to suicide or injury during suicide attempts, or to alleged impropriety, including sexual impropriety, by the treating professional. Many plaintiff's attorneys pursue a policy of initially suing all the health care workers named in the chart of a client with a negative outcome; fortunately, those clinicians who did not actually practice negligently often are dismissed as defendants during the course of litigation as it becomes clear that their actions did not contribute to the plaintiff's bad clinical outcome.

An area of practice specifically pertaining to addictions that can result in malpractice claims is the inappropriate prescription of addictive medications to patients who are susceptible to substance dependence. Addiction psychiatrists should be particularly careful in prescribing narcotic pain medications, psychostimulants, and abusable sedative-hypnotics to their patients with substance-related disorders, because a previous history of abuse of one substance can be predictive of the likelihood of a patient's abusing another one. Addiction psychiatrists should obtain clear informed consent from their patients indicating that the patients understand the addictive properties of their medication (Gendel 2004). Of course, like all health care workers, clinicians who treat substance-abusing patients should maintain proper records of their patients' care.

It is important that clinicians have access to guidance by an attorney when they encounter tricky issues in their practice, including when there is a risk of a malpractice suit. If a suit is filed, legal advice sought early can improve the outcome for the treatment professional.

Conclusion

All mental health and addiction treatment clinicians need to be aware of the potential legal involvement of their patients. Clinicians who treat addicted persons may encounter many patients who lead lives marked by violence and poor impulse control. Knowing some basics of civil and criminal law allows addiction treatment professionals to best help their patients overcome their illnesses and lead useful lives.

Core Concepts

- Addiction treatment professionals frequently encounter legal issues in their everyday practice.

- Knowledge of the laws pertaining to coerced treatment of substance-dependent patients is important in the practice of addiction treatment.

- Patients in addiction treatment frequently have involvement in both the civil and criminal legal systems.

Important Areas of Interaction between Addiction Treatment and Civil Law

- Court orders for the treatment of addiction
- Civil competency to make personal and financial decisions
- Disability from alcohol and drug dependence
- Confidentiality and the duty to protect the public from the actions of addicted individuals
- Malpractice in addiction psychiatry

Important Areas of Interaction between Addiction Treatment and Criminal Law

- Competency of substance-abusing individuals to stand trial in criminal cases
- Insanity defenses in addicted patients
- The relationship of specific intent in criminal cases to substance abuse

Essentials for Clinicians Dealing with Legal Issues in Addiction Treatment

- Knowledge of the status of voluntary and involuntary treatment for alcoholism and drug dependence in the clinician's jurisdiction
- Understanding the principles of confidentiality of treatment records and limitations on confidentiality
- Availability of legal consultation when questions arise or when a malpractice suit may occur

Case Examples	Core Concepts
Carly is a thirty-five-year-old woman who has a previous history of alcohol dependence but has been abstinent for one year while under the care of an addiction psychiatrist. Carly develops symptoms of panic disorder and is treated with oral clonazepam. The psychiatrist fails to obtain clear written informed consent from Carly regarding the potentially addictive nature of clonazepam; Carly increases the dose of clonazepam on her own and becomes dependent on it. Carly then sues the addiction psychiatrist, alleging that he failed to take into account her susceptibility to addiction. The psychiatrist unwisely alters Carly's medical record to indicate that he did not know of her history of substance dependence. The psychiatrist is caught and disciplined by his state's medical licensing board for falsifying Carly's record, and he faces a serious claim of malpractice in prescribing an addictive substance without adequate informed consent.	Importance of informed consent to treatment

Importance of maintaining an accurate health care record |
| Sam, a twenty-eight-year-old man with a six-year history of methamphetamine dependence, stopped using cocaine one year ago and has been under the care of an addiction psychiatrist since then for a substance-induced psychosis. Sam has continued to experience auditory hallucinations and persecutory delusions during the past year, despite abstinence from methamphetamine and other illegal drugs and alcohol. The intensity of his hallucinations and delusions has been reduced by treatment with ziprasidone.

Sam believes that his neighbor is listening to his telephone calls through a device in the neighbor's kitchen. Acting in response to his delusions, Sam throws a stone through the neighbor's kitchen window. Sam, who lives in a state that uses the M'Naughten Test for insanity, is charged with criminal damage to property.

Sam pleads insanity on the basis of his substance-induced psychosis. He tells the evaluating psychiatrist that he knew it was wrong to throw the rock through the neighbor's window, but that the voices he heard compelled him to do it. The evaluating psychiatrist writes a report stating her opinion that, although the defendant (Sam) suffered at the time of the offense from a real psychosis that has persisted long after he stopped abusing methamphetamine, the defendant is not eligible for the insanity defense in a state using the M'Naughten Test because, by his own admission, he knew the wrongfulness of his criminal action. | Clinical significance of persistent psychotic symptoms in abstinent patients with a history of psychostimulant dependence

Cognitive basis of M'Naughten Test for insanity defense: knowledge by the defendant at the time of his defense of the nature and wrongfulness of his actions |

Recommended Readings

Gendel, M. H. 2004. Forensic and medical legal issues in addiction psychiatry. *Psychiatric Clinics of North America* 27:614–19.

Hardy, D. W., M. Patel, and D. Paull. 2000. Basic law for addiction psychiatry. *Psychiatric Annals* 30 (9): 574–80.

Mack, A. H., and H. A. Lightdale. 2006. Forensic addiction psychiatry for the clinician, the expert, and the in-between. *Addictive Disorders and Their Treatment* 5 (2): 80–81.

Ethical Issues in the Treatment of Women
with Substance Abuse

DIANE T. CASTILLO, PH.D.
V. ANN WALDORF, PH.D.

Clinicians treating women with substance abuse diagnoses face unique ethical challenges. The goal of this chapter is to identify for clinicians some of these potential ethical pitfalls and offer suggestions for avoiding them in therapeutic work with patients. Background information will first be provided in the form of general stereotypes and risk factors for women substance abusers in our culture, as these stereotypes are often the foundations that influence discrimination of women who abuse substances. Self-awareness and the influence of stereotypes in the clinician are key in approaching the female substance-abusing patient ethically. General bioethical principles facing the clinician will be outlined and followed with an application of these principles to treating women with substance use disorders within a framework of a current model of sexism. Case examples will be used to demonstrate the expression of potential ethics violations within the application of bioethics and stereotyping of substance-abusing women. The chapter will conclude with core concepts and recommended readings to further aid clinicians.

Stereotyping of Women

When working with any female patient, substance abusing or not, it is important to be aware of sexism, which, despite some progress, continues to exist in American culture. One form of sexism for women in American society has its roots in viewing women in a dichotomous fashion, with extremely positive stereo-types of the woman as everyone's mother/wife/sister, which puts women on a pedestal. The other extreme stereotype includes the immensely negative idea of the woman as prostitute/bad girl in the gutter. This historical dualistic classification is limiting, in that it places our views of women in either of these two extreme categories and does not allow for viewing the diversity of women as humans with a variety of experiences, such as sexuality, with-out resulting in a judgmental stance. While it is certainly extreme to view women in this either/or fashion and does not likely reflect the views of most clinicians, its roots in our society may subtly influence our views of women, particularly those women who struggle with alcohol or drug addiction. More often than not, addicts or substance-using women may be perceived in a way that emphasizes negative stereotypes.

Another framework for conceptualizing society's treatment of women based on a dichotomy was offered by Glick (2001), in which the polar extremes are labeled as hostile versus benevolent sexism. The more familiar form of sexism is hostile sexism and is defined as "an adversarial view of gender relations in which women are perceived as seeking to control men, whether through sexuality or feminist ideology" (109). Because of its overt hostility, this type of sexism is more likely to be offensive to women, and is especially more obvious in more modern cultures. Benevolent sexism, which may coexist with hostile sexism, views women as "pure creatures who ought to be protected, supported, and adored and whose love is necessary to make a man complete" (109). This type of sexism may seem less controlling of women, and as such is more likely to be endorsed by men and women and is more socially accepted. However, benevolent sexism can also result in gender inequality because it implies that women are weak and suited for more conventional roles. Benevolent sexism can be viewed as a form of paternalism and promotes dominance by men in the culture. Although the authors acknowledge lower rates of sexism in clinical settings, a greater awareness of the origins of these stereotypes and sexism will ensure that clinicians maintain objectivity in their work with women who present with substance abuse problems.

Stereotyping of Substance Abusers

In addition to gender stereotyping, the perception of women with substance abuse issues is compounded by the stereotypical views prevalent about any person struggling with problematic substance use. It has been shown (Cohen, Griffin, and Wiltz 1982) that nonaddicts view addicts as severely ill, having little control over their lives, and hostile and anxious. While mental health professionals' views of addicts in general may tend to be less harsh than those of the general public (and stereotyping tends to decrease with more education), the medical students and residents in the study also viewed addicts as more anxious and in less control of their lives than non-substance-using peers. Because substance abusers in general are viewed more negatively by society and even by some clinicians, we can assume these negative perceptions are also applied to substance-abusing women. This combination of stereotyping for gender and substance abuse often ensures that women who abuse substances face some of the harshest societal judgment. The most negative ideas are associated with females who abuse illicit drugs. These individuals are consistently viewed more negatively than either females who abuse alcohol or males who abuse any substance.

Risk Factors for Substance-abusing Women

To fully appreciate the impact of stereotyping, it is important to be familiar with risk factors affecting the likelihood of substance abuse in women. About 5 percent of American women meet the criteria for alcohol abuse or dependence, while 1.5 percent are abusing or dependent on illicit, nonalcoholic drugs (Goldberg 1995). By race, the rate of alcoholism is high among Native American women. However, white women have been found to drink more heavily when compared with African American or

Hispanic women. Although the stereotype is that female substance abusers are poor, nonwhite women, similar rates of substance abuse have been found in affluent white samples for total drug use when compared with other groups. This is particularly interesting because it has been shown that women of color with children are more likely than white women to be tested for drug use and referred to child protective services. In an overall comparison with men, women are less likely to abuse alcohol and illicit substances but are more likely to abuse prescription medication, such as tranquilizers and diet pills.

Other factors more commonly found among females make some more vulnerable to developing a substance use disorder. Goldberg (1995) identified childhood and adult sexual violence, including domestic violence, as two of these factors. The lifetime prevalence of sexual assault for women ranges from 18 percent to 44 percent (Casey and Nurius 2006), whereas in men it ranges from 2 percent to 14 percent. Women also are more likely to be the victims of domestic violence, which is the largest source of injuries and hospitalizations in women in the United States. Adult female victims of domestic violence have a higher rate of substance abuse than women who are not victims. Compounded with gender-specific risk factors, it has been found that an individual with a history of childhood physical abuse who also has one or both parents with alcohol dependence has an increased risk of substance abuse when compared with an individual who does not have those factors.

Goldberg (1995) defines other risk factors in women that further enhance the risk of becoming abusers of or addicted to substances as compared with men. These include, but are not limited to, continued discrimination in the workforce in terms of hiring, pay, and promotion. Another striking comparison shows that not only are women who abuse substances more likely to be left by a male partner, but also women are more likely to begin abusing substances if left by a partner, even if the behavior was not problematic prior to the partner's departure.

Other special issues faced by women, as outlined by Roberts and Dunn (2003), are worth mentioning because they are unique to women; they include barriers to treatment, responsibility for children, and the care of pregnant substance-abusing women. Most available treatments for substance abuse problems may necessarily exclude women, because women are the primary caretakers for children. Treatment programs, whether inpatient or outpatient, do not account for child care needs, and therefore either substance-abusing women are excluded or treatment may be prematurely terminated. This barrier to treatment is not faced by the male substance-abusing counterpart and is not typically acknowledged by the mental health community. Women who are primary caretakers for children and who abuse substances face greater judgment and scrutiny by the public and mental health community for neglect of their children, issues not applied to their male counterparts.

Treating substance-abusing women who are pregnant presents additional ethical issues because of the effects of substances on the fetus (Roberts and Dunn 2003; Jos, Perlmutter, and Marshall 2003; Tillett and Osborne 2000). The ethical dilemma raises the question of whose rights are to be protected—those of the pregnant woman as an individual or of the fetus as a separate entity. Presently, thirty-five states have prosecuted pregnant women who have abused alcohol or drugs during pregnancy for "child abuse" (Jos, Perlmutter, and Marshall 2003) and have forced medical professionals to participate through mandatory reporting requirements. Professional associations have opposed these actions, and the focus has shifted ethics from the clinical encounter to a public health model. At the heart of the "individual versus fetus rights" debate is the issue of abortion (Tillett and Osborne 2000), which draws into the arena public opinion by right-to-life advocates. Roberts and Dunn (2003) report that, although the negative effect of alcohol and tobacco on the fetus is well established, the effects of other drugs and drug combinations on the fetus are complicated by factors such as socioeconomic status, education, and poor nutrition. There is no clear direction for the clinician in addressing the ethics that emerge in treating the pregnant substance-abusing female, but the issues to be addressed concern confidentiality, beneficence, autonomy, and justice. For a full review, see Roberts and Dunn (2003).

Bioethical Principles

Given the profound bias often associated with addictions in women, a thorough understanding of bioethical principles that must underlie substance use treatment is necessary. Roberts and Dunn (2003) have provided a five-domain framework that can assist clinicians in focusing on key ethical principles that Roberts had previously identified as vital to the care of women with substance use disorders: (1) voluntarism; (2) beneficence, compassion, and harm reduction; (3) confidentiality and truth telling; (4) respect for persons and justice; and (5) informed consent.

Voluntarism reflects the level at which a patient has the ability to act with autonomy in decisions of care. As Roberts and Dunn (2003) suggest, this is particularly complex given the numerous factors associated with such decision making in a population that has often demonstrated an impaired capacity to control substance use despite a desire and an understanding of deleterious consequences.

Beneficence reflects the ethical obligation of clinicians to promote the well-being of patients, including females who abuse substances. Compassion reflects the appreciation for and understanding of the plight of the patient, and harm reduction represents attempts to minimize the negative effects experienced by the patient.

Confidentiality and truth telling reflect the obligation of clinicians to maintain the information disclosed in the medical/therapeutic setting as private. Specific to individuals with substance use disorders, many patients' actions may directly violate the law, especially in the case of illegal substance use. Truth telling is essential as the clinician outlines the limits of confidentiality and professional constraints such as the need to report when the patient is a danger to herself and/or others and particularly when elder and/or child abuse is suspected. The clinician may interpret child abuse narrowly or more broadly, as outlined earlier in the chapter, and may violate confidentiality by interpreting substance abuse, particularly of illegal substances, as child abuse and reporting patients to authorities. It is the clinician's responsibility, therefore, to examine the potential for personal moral values conflicting with ethical obligations to the patient.

Respect for persons reflects "a genuine consideration and attentiveness to the person's life history, values, and goals" (Roberts and Dunn 2003:561). Justice reflects the obligation of fairness and equal treatment in the offering of services. Given the illegality of some substances and the stigma and stereotypes associated with substance abusers, the clinician is again compelled to examine personal morals and values in order to comply with ethical obligations.

Finally, informed consent revolves around ensuring that patients are fully aware of the treatment options available to them and of the nature of their illnesses. Informed consent is not a stagnant, single event but, rather, is viewed as a process that changes and continually involves interaction between provider and patient. As a substance abuser, the patient is likely to demonstrate varying levels of comprehension regarding treatment requirements and options, depending on her stage of growth in treatment, and thus the clinician needs to continually inform the patient of treatment procedures and options.

Most clinicians likely adhere to the bioethical principles outlined above when they approach the treatment of women with substance use disorders. However, it is possible, given the prevalence of stereotypical beliefs previously mentioned, that an individual clinician's cultural biases might unwittingly affect the application of these principles in subtle ways. The remainder of the chapter will juxtapose Glick's (2001) framework of hostile versus benevolent sexism and Roberts and Dunn's (2003) domains for treatment in an effort to expose potential problems that embedded beliefs may pose to the ethical treatment of this patient population in even the most sincere provider.

Sexism and the Ethical Domains

The interface of hostile and benevolent sexism with specific ethical factors is outlined in Figure 7.1, Bioethical Principles and Hostile/Benevolent Sexism with Female Substance Abusers. For example, hostile sexism within voluntarism could underlie an overestimation of the patient's autonomy. If a provider assumes that the patient is capable of making effective choices, despite evidence to the contrary in her use patterns, that provider may confer greater responsibility to the patient than appropriate. In comparison, benevolent sexism in voluntarism might be evident in the minimization of the patient's ability to make choices with a risk of infantilizing her and giving her less accountability than would be clinically effective.

Beneficence can be affected by types of sexism. Although a clinician may well be promoting the client's best interest, hostile sexism can result in a patronizing attitude that leaves the patient cared for but without an experience of compassion and empathy. Within benevolent sexism, the clinician might overidentify with the patient's traumatic circumstance, losing objectivity in providing services and not effectively engaging the patient when actual change talk is observed.

Confidentiality, which at first glance appears to be relatively straightforward, is also fraught with potential pitfalls should a clinician not be fully aware of sexist attitudes influencing the work with a female client. With hostile sexism, the clinician may assume a more dogmatic stance in reporting abuse without simultaneously appreciating the impact of that reporting on the therapeutic alliance. On the other hand, with benevolent sexism a clinician might take a subjective approach, which takes into account progress made with regard to decreased frequency or severity of abuse, and actually fail to report necessary violations.

FIGURE 7.1

**Bioethical Principles and Hostile/Benevolent Sexism
with Female Substance Abusers**

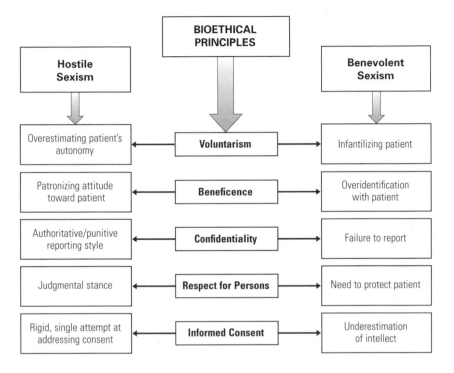

Although one might assume that respect for persons is inherent in the care of substance abusers, this is not necessarily the case. For example, it is not uncommon for providers to have a markedly different view of an individual based solely on that person's drug of choice. Compounding that with the stereotypes that have been outlined, it is not difficult to imagine a scenario in which a clinician's respect for persons is impaired by hostile sexism when there is an acceptance of the negative stereotypes about certain types of female substance abusers, such as a crack cocaine addict with children in the home. Even benevolent sexism may result in pitfalls for the treating provider. In much the same way as with voluntarism, if the provider only sees the client as a victim of her circumstance or upbringing, the tendency is to rescue the individual without respecting the fact that the harmful decisions she is making are still her prerogative.

Finally, with the informed consent process there also are risks with either type of sexism present. The hostile sexism pitfall is failing to view informed consent as the dynamic process that it is. Instead, the clinician may take a "facts only" approach, failing to appreciate subtle changes in the client's capacity to appreciate the effects of consent over time and the course of treatment. Benevolent sexism could result in an underestimation of the woman's intellectual capacity in light of her emotionality, thereby limiting the opportunity for the process-oriented approach.

Sexism Case Illustrations

The following are two case examples from the authors' own work that demonstrate the ways in which sexism of either stripe can happen when a clinician is not constantly vigilant. This sexism affects ongoing psychotherapy in these patients.

Case 1

Gayle is a fifty-year-old divorced Hispanic female who first presented for treatment for post-traumatic stress disorder (PTSD). She was raised in a traditional Hispanic family with little experience outside her small, tightly knit circle of family and church friends. She married young to a man several years her senior who was the manager of the retail store where she got a job out of high school. Her marriage was marked by multiple incidents of domestic violence and profound social isolation that extended to the couple's child. After her child was grown and out of the home, she divorced her husband and has attempted to function independently, with only limited success. She lives alone, has minimal contact with remaining family, who know little of her domestic violence history, and struggles with an overwhelming sense of failure. Her substance abuse includes both alcohol and prescription drugs. Although she had no experience with either prior to her marriage, her former husband often used substances as a way to control her. Over time, she reports, substances enabled her to "go away from all the pain and despair."

The authors' work with this individual, for the treatment of both PTSD and polysubstance dependence, required constant vigilance to ensure that voluntarism, beneficence, and respect for persons did not become negatively affected by a type of benevolent sexism. One specific example was with the level of voluntarism that was granted the patient. The extent of her true victimization in the past was often a concern, as the individual was encouraged to challenge herself to attempt behaviors that, although therapeutic, were terribly anxiety-producing. These assignments were often experienced by the patient as "another thing that was being forced on her," despite the fact that she could enunciate the ways that this therapeutic assignment was necessary for her recovery. This situation was further complicated by the authors' knowledge that this patient's anxiety and perceived victimization often heightened her risk of relapse.

Case 2

Michelle is a forty-two-year-old divorced white female who originally presented for treatment approximately fifteen years ago for opiate abuse, PTSD, and borderline personality disorder. Additionally, she receives Social Security Disability and Worker's Compensation for a work-related injury sustained in her early twenties and reports chronic pain with little abatement despite numerous invasive and noninvasive procedures. Unlike the earlier case, this patient had a profoundly disrupted childhood marked by both physical and sexual abuse, neglect, and abandonment. She "ran off to get married to get away from all that," only to find herself in another abusive relationship with a substance-abusing husband. Following multiple interactions with local law enforcement officers that resulted in forced hospitalizations, the client eventually lost custody of her two young daughters. She came for treatment shortly after their permanent removal to state custody.

Although it might be suspected that the authors' interactions with this individual would trigger the same benevolent sexism as the earlier case, this has not been their experience. Despite the cognitive understanding of the role of childhood trauma in the client's presentation, her current inability to move beyond a pervasive sense of self as victim has at times required additional effort on the part of the clinicians to ensure no hostile sexism in the areas of beneficence, confidentiality, and respect for persons. A specific example in this case would be confidentiality. The patient has made repeated threats of suicide, often in conjunction with unwillingness on the part of her treating physicians to provide early narcotic refills. Although the patient does have serious suicide attempts in her remote history, none have occurred while she has received care at our facility. And yet, the decision to break confidentiality and call for an involuntary pickup during her periods of exacerbation always requires careful analysis of risk versus an effort to curb the tendency to make the threat without intent.

Conclusion

Women who abuse substances enter treatment rife with cultural stereotyping. They struggle against dichotomous views of women that race and family circumstance only exacerbate. Additionally, they carry the baggage of society's views of substance users that, although complex, may be based on something as singular as the drug of choice. Both of these characteristics, female and substance abuser, have a documented history of eliciting particular responses in members of our society, and clinicians cannot assume that their own work is not influenced by this history. Although others have provided a clear framework for providing ethical treatment, it is important to remember that those guidelines are being applied by clinicians who bring to the therapeutic dynamic their own experience of females and substance abusers outside the clinical setting. This chapter attempts to heighten the awareness of all clinicians—even well-trained practitioners with the most honorable intentions—to the fact that there is always the potential for a misstep in the ethical treatment of female patients. However, with constant vigilance to both ethical practice guidelines and the subtle manifestation of one's own sexism, it is hoped that only a misstep might occur and not a full fall into an ethical pit.

Core Concepts

• Within voluntarism, hostile sexism could underlie an overestimation of the patient's autonomy; benevolent sexism might result in minimizing the patient's ability to make choices with a risk of infantilizing her and giving her less accountability than would be clinically effective.

• A patronizing attitude can leave the patient cared for but without an experience of compassion and empathy.

• Clinicians may overidentify with the patient, lose objectivity in providing services, and not effectively engage the patient.

• The clinician may assume a more dogmatic stance in reporting abuse without simultaneously appreciating the impact of that reporting on the therapeutic alliance. Alternatively, a clinician might take into account progress made to decreased frequency or severity of abuse and fail to report necessary violations.

• Providers may have a markedly different view of an individual based solely on that person's drug of choice.

• Informed consent is a dynamic process that requires more than a "facts only" approach and not underestimating the woman's intellectual capacity in light of her emotionality, thereby limiting the opportunity for the process-oriented approach.

Case Examples	Core Concepts
Louise, a fifty-year-old divorced Hispanic female, has severe PTSD and polysubstance dependence.	The extent of traumas may engender benevolent sexism in determining the course of treatment.
Rox, a thirty-six-year-old single female African American, is a homeless heroin addict and prostitute.	The respect for persons is challenged in the clinician due to illegal behaviors and/or cultural stereotypes (hostile sexism).
Pamela, a thirty-year-old polysubstance abuser, is also a mother of three kids under ten years of age. Pamela is referred by the court system for treatment.	A question arises of breaching confidentiality around neglect of children and judging client behaviors (hostile sexism).
Lee, a twenty-five-year-old single pregnant female, abuses alcohol, cigarettes, and marijuana.	The clinician is challenged to examine personal biases in determination of whether mom or fetus is patient (hostile or benevolent sexism).
Amanda, a forty-eight-year-old married, affluent white female mother of three, abuses prescription pain and anxiety medications.	There is a potential to presume the client is aware of the consequences of the consent process to issues of custody (benevolent sexism).

Recommended Readings

Glick, P. 2001. An ambivalent alliance: Hostile and benevolent sexism as complementary justifications for gender inequality. *American Psychologist* 56 (2): 109–18.

Roberts, L. W., and L. B. Dunn. 2003. Ethical considerations in caring for women with substance use disorders. *Obstetrics and Gynecology Clinics of North America* 30:559–82.

8

Ethical Aspects of the Treatment of Substance Abuse in Children and Adolescents

JERALD BELITZ, PH.D.

Numerous health factors that negatively influence the health status of Americans have direct implications for adolescents, including tobacco use, substance abuse, sexual activity, mental health, injury prevention, and access to health care (Olds 2003). The Surgeon General (DHHS 2004) concludes that tobacco use is the single-greatest cause of disease and that 22 percent of youths smoke cigarettes. At any given time, 9.9 percent of youths use an illicit drug (Office of National Drug Control Policy 2007).

The National Institute on Alcohol Abuse and Alcoholism (NIAAA 2004/2005a) identifies the deleterious consequences of underage drinking as increased risk of depression, suicide, homicide, sexual and physical assault, unintended and unprotected sex, dropping out of school, medical problems, alterations in brain development and cognitive capabilities, death from motor vehicle crashes and other unintended injuries, and increased risk of tobacco and drug abuse. More specifically, alcohol use contributes to 35 percent of adolescent fatalities in motor vehicle crashes and 40 percent of adolescent drownings. Youths who use alcohol are twice as likely to commit suicide as their nonusing peers. It is estimated that 2.6 million adolescents require treatment for severe alcohol or drug problems; however, fewer than 7 percent of these youths receive therapeutic services (Waldron et al. 2007). Clearly, an overwhelming number of adolescents are not accessing health care for their substance abuse and are at significant risk of additional harm.

Reports by the Surgeon General (DHHS 2001a, 2001b) identify substance abuse as a significant behavioral and medical health problem for children and adolescents and call for additional research to identify efficacious and effective treatments. Treatment and research with minors, especially those who engage in substance abuse, create a crossroads where multiple forces intersect to generate multiple ethical quandaries. Clinicians and researchers must be knowledgeable about relevant state and federal laws, standards of practice and professionalism, their own values and biases, developmental aspects of youth and adolescence, and the ecological and contextual environments in which youths live and function.

Clinical Treatment Issues

Ethical themes related to the treatment of minors include informed consent, confidentiality, evidence-based practices, familial and cultural elements, and professional competence. All of these issues are confounded by substance abuse, a behavior that is considered illegal by virtue of age and/or by use of an illicit substance. An ongoing tension exists among the rights of the youth, of the family, and of the community.

Informed Consent

Informed consent is viewed as the cornerstone of ethical health care (Kuther 2003). Providers recognize the individual patient's dignity, autonomy, and capacity for self-determination. Within the context of the provider-patient relationship, the clinician and patient collaboratively determine the course of treatment. Before a patient's consent can be considered informed, the individual must understand the risks and benefits of accepting or declining the treatment and the potential outcomes of alternative treatments, possess decisional capacity, and provide a voluntary and noncoerced decision.

Historically, minors were regarded as incapable of supplying informed consent, and the responsibility for health decisions was ascribed to their parents or legal guardians. In recent years, legislators, clinicians, and researchers have recognized the construct of a mature minor, a youth who possesses the requisite cognitive and emotional abilities to provide informed consent. A substantial body of research (Kuther 2003) demonstrates that by age fourteen, minors have emotional maturity, cognitive capabilities, and decisional capabilities equal to those of adults. These minors exhibit the ability to understand factual issues, potential outcomes, the consequences of each alternative, and the meaning of the decision within the framework of their personal values. In response to this data, all fifty states have passed legislation that allows mature minors the authority to consent to specific health care decisions related to contraceptives, pregnancy, sexually transmitted diseases, mental health, or substance abuse. Forty-four states and the District of Columbia have statutes that allow a mature minor to consent to confidential treatment for alcohol and substance abuse (Boonstra and Nash 2000).

In a position paper (Ford, English, and Sigman 2004) that delineates the principles of confidential health care for adolescents, the Society for Adolescent Medicine (SAM) accentuates the fundamental necessity of allowing adolescents to consent to their own treatment, particularly for sensitive health concerns. SAM emphasizes that adolescents will either abstain from health care or will provide incomplete and less than honest information if they are not assured of confidentiality. Essentially, those adolescents who engage in substance use and the illegal and high-risk behaviors associated with it (e.g., addiction, unprotected sexual activity, crime) are the least likely to access care. By allowing adolescents to consent to confidential treatment, the ethical standards of patient autonomy, beneficence, nonmaleficence, and justice are honored.

There is research that questions the capacity of mature minors to provide informed consent independently (Kuther 2003). Age is an arbitrary means of demarcating when a youth becomes decisionally competent; not all adolescents achieve developmental milestones at the same rate or sequence. Adolescents' capacity to provide voluntary consent may be altered by the complexity of the decision, the effect of authority figures or peers, the context of their own personal experiences, and their current emotional status. Much of the research attesting to a minor's decisional capabilities has occurred in laboratory settings and may not generalize to real-world settings, where a minor may not have all the relevant information afforded in a research environment.

Important to recognize is that the use of substances can damage or compromise a youth's cognitive ability to furnish informed consent (Brody and Waldron 2000). Cognitive deficits are common during periods of intoxication and withdrawal. Substance abuse has been associated with cognitive impairments in the areas of attention, concentration, processing of information, motivation, and perception. Substance-abusing minors may not have the decisional capacity of their nonabusing peers.

Brody and Waldron (2000) astutely observe that many minors are referred to treatment by parents, school officials, juvenile justice personnel, or other representatives of their social system only after their substance-abusing behaviors have been discerned. These youths may consent to health care because an individual or system exerts power by denying them access to school or other social and legal privileges unless they receive the required treatment. Though it is in the adolescents' best interest to receive care, this does not meet the standard for voluntarism.

Essentially, health care providers are encouraged to assess their historical relationship with the individual youth and family and to assess the youth's chronological age, psychosocial level of development, and current health status and health-related behaviors before determining the youth's decisional capacity.

Confidentiality

Confidential information can only be disclosed to a third party with the authorization of the individual who provided informed consent for the treatment. Typically the legal guardian is the minor's personal representative and possesses this privilege; however, when a mature minor is legally sanctioned to supply consent to substance abuse treatment, that minor is granted the legal right to consent to or refuse the release of confidential information. This protection of confidentiality also precludes releasing information to the legal guardian without the adolescent's authorization. These statutes recognize that adolescents will neither access necessary care nor honestly engage in treatment if they are not assured of this confidentiality. This avoidance of care has negative health implications for both the individual youth and for the larger issue of public health. In the event that state law does not explicitly detail the mature minor's confidential rights, the Health Insurance Portability and Accountability Act of 1996 (HIPAA) privacy rules prevail; the independently licensed health care professional, acting in the best interest of the minor, has the authority to determine if and when the guardian will have access to protected information.

Virtually every state has provisions that permit health care providers to bypass the requirement of a mature minor's authorized releases of information. Providers may disclose protected health information to other clinicians or concerned individuals if that information is considered vital for the continuity of care for that youth or vital for the protection of that youth, others, or the public against imminent harm (English and Ford 2004). Health care providers are expected to ensure the safety of all their minor patients and are legally required to report any suspected child abuse to an identified state agency. Providers have a responsibility to explain their specific limits of confidentiality, based on state and federal laws and professional standards and ethics, and to explain their clinical definitions of imminent harm and the best interest of the minor at the initiation of services and again whenever it is clinically or developmentally appropriate. This is particularly salient for substance-abusing adolescents because of their higher incidences of suicide and homicide, driving while intoxicated and causing either their own or another's death, death by other accidents caused by their intoxication, or dangerous activities related to the procuring of illegal substances.

Minors also can be afforded a degree of confidentiality when they lack the legal status to consent to their own treatment. This requires the guardian to assent to an agreement of confidentiality between the minor and clinician, thereby permitting the minor to function as the individual who authorizes the release of information (English and Ford 2004). However, this is not stipulated in any statutes, and the clinician is obligated to act in the best interest of the minor. Such an agreement is especially useful when the youth receives treatment as the result of demands from juvenile justice or school officials. Even though the adolescent consents to the treatment, albeit under duress, the referring agency may expect ongoing reports pertaining to the youth's attendance, motivation, progress, or results from drug screens. Clinicians harvest information about the adolescent's substance use and associated behaviors that can lead to a therapeutic placement outside the home, expulsion from school, or incarceration and other penalties from the courts. Brody and Waldron (2000) caution that disclosure of such confidential material can cause harm to the youth. They suggest that clinicians agree to disclose only the youth's level of attendance to the referring agencies. As noted above, the clinician will adhere to the policies that permit and require breach of confidentiality and will act in the best interest of the minor.

Another potential violation of confidentiality relates to billing and third-party reimbursement practices. Customarily, bills are transmitted to either the guardian or a health insurance carrier, and protected information can be disclosed to the guardian unintentionally through data on the bill or explanations of benefits. It is not uncommon for the juvenile justice system or other social agencies to mandate substance abuse treatment and remunerate the clinician, allowing the payer to either solicit protected information or inadvertently receive that information. Providers are encouraged to work with the minor and third-party payers to restrict the information that is conveyed in the billing procedures. Or providers can offer services at a discounted fee or refer the minor to a community resource that furnishes free or affordable care.

Family Involvement in Treatment

Although adolescents are afforded the right to consent to confidential care, it may be in their best interest to include family members in the treatment process. The research literature confirms the effectiveness of family-based therapies in reducing adolescent substance abuse and improving family functioning (NIAAA 2004/2005b). This may not be the preference of adolescents who request confidential services, but it is a robust option for youths who are court ordered or referred by a social agency for treatment.

At the onset of treatment, the clinician determines whether the youth or the family is the patient and clarifies professional relationships with the various family members, including guidelines regarding the release of confidential information. Potential problems related to documentation and record keeping are also proactively clarified. Because it is not uncommon for sensitive information about family members to be included in the youth's chart, clinicians need to educate family members about the procedures that protect each member's confidentiality. This is a particular vulnerability when a third party is mandating or financing the treatment. Measures to protect against unintended disclosures include maintaining separate records for each family member, documenting data only about the identified patient, securing distinct releases of information for each member, or deleting sensitive material from the record before discharging it to a third party.

Evidence-based Treatments

Is it ethical for a provider to utilize interventions that lack empirical evidence? Is it ethical to utilize evidence-based therapies with populations that were not included in the clinical trials? Although there is an increase in the citations for evidence-based interventions, many lack specificity with regard to the patient's age, gender, ethnicity, or culture. The NIAAA (2004/2005b) reports that many services are not designed for youth access or engagement and lack attention to developmental issues. While adult addiction programs are often used with adolescents, they have not been empirically evaluated with nonadult populations.

Interventions that have empirical evidence incorporate developmental aspects. They include individual and group cognitive-behavioral therapies that focus on coping skills and self-regulation (Waldron and Kaminer 2004) and family-based therapies, specifically multisystemic therapy (Swensen et al. 2005), multidimensional family therapy (Liddle 2004), and strategic family therapy (Szapocznik, Hervis, and Schwartz 2003). These family interventions have achieved success with minority populations. A family-based intervention that focuses on parenting skills, community reinforcement, and family training has emerging evidence of effectiveness (Waldron et al. 2007). The NIAAA (2004/2005b) further cites motivational interviewing and psychopharmacological interventions for co-occurring disorders as promising treatments.

Methadone therapy is rarely approved for adolescents; however, there is evidence that buprenorphine replacement therapy is beneficial for older adolescents with opioid dependence (Levy et al. 2007). This is especially true when the intervention is matched with parental involvement and behavior therapies.

Professional Competence

Clinicians are ethically compelled to practice within the scope of their professional competencies. Health care providers who work with substance-abusing youth are obliged to comprehend normal and abnormal development in the domains of cognitive, moral, emotional, social, and self-regulatory processes. They are further advised to understand the ecological context in which development occurs, including the variables of family, culture, ethnicity, religious beliefs, socioeconomics, schools, peers, and biology. It is requisite that clinicians are cognizant of the developmental and contextual elements that contribute to substance abuse and dependency and that clinicians are proficient in utilizing interventions that are evidence-based and developmentally appropriate for youths.

Professional competence also demands that providers appraise their own attitudes and morals about substance abuse and the individuals who abuse those substances. Much stigma is associated with substance abuse, and clinicians are urged to analyze any potential biases that may reinforce that stigma or obstruct the therapeutic process. This involves examining conceptualizations about the etiology of substance abuse, the rights of minors to consent to confidential treatment, and the role of the family in treatment. Self-awareness of one's own history with substance use (personal use and use by significant others) can prevent clinicians from imposing their perspective onto the patient and not attending to the unique needs and strengths of the patient. Finally, clinicians are encouraged to assess whether their treatment objectives for youths incorporate a model of abstinence or of harm reduction. If there is incongruency between the provider and patient, the youth can be referred to another professional who is better able to match interventions with that particular minor.

Research Issues

In 1998, the National Institutes of Health (NIH 1998) called for the participation of minors in research that investigates the treatment of childhood disorders. This research is intended to benefit youths who are diagnosed with specific disorders and to improve the public health status of minors. Research with youths, especially those who engage in illegal behaviors, generates complex ethical questions and challenges. Again, there is a dynamic tension among the rights of the youth, the rights of the family, and the rights of the community.

Informed Consent and Confidentiality

Minors are identified as a vulnerable population by the U.S. Department of Health and Human Services (DHHS 1983) and consequently need safety measures to protect their rights and to protect them from undue harm. DHHS balances the risks to the minor with the benefits to the individual participant and the knowledge that can be generated to better understand or treat other children with the same disorder. Minimal risk is defined as exposure to events no greater than those typically experienced in a minor's daily life. In circumstances that pose more than a minimal risk, minors cannot be exposed to any events that are not congruent with those experienced in routine medical, dental, psychological, social, or educational situations.

Parents and guardians are afforded the right to provide "permission" for their children to participate in research. Information about the research is presented to minors at a level compatible with their age and developmental level, and minors then must assent, or affirmatively agree, to participate. Minors retain the right to decline to participate. More recently, federal regulations (Diviak et al. 2004) established criteria by which Institutional Review Boards (IRBs) can waive the parental permission requirement and, thereby, allow minors to consent to confidential participation in research. All three of the following conditions must be present: the research involves no more than minimal risk, the waiver of parental permission will not adversely affect the welfare of the research participant, and the research project could not be practically carried out without the waiver of parental permission. In reality, it is quite difficult to solicit this waiver from IRBs. A review of twelve funded smoking cessation studies (Diviak et al. 2004) revealed that only four IRBs waived parental permission and allowed the adolescent participants to independently provide assent without any additional stipulations.

In states where mature minors have the right to consent to their own confidential substance abuse treatment, IRBs may waive the parental permission requirement and allow the adolescents to consent to their participation in confidential treatment research. Diviak and colleagues (2004) discovered that two of the researchers who received this waiver from an IRB referenced their relevant state laws.

SAM (Santelli et al. 2003) modified the three guiding principles of ethical research—autonomy, beneficence, and justice—to produce a code that is applicable to research with adolescent populations. The principle of autonomy, or respect for personhood, is defined as honoring the dignity and right of self-determination of each research participant. This respect extends to the families of the youths and to the communities in which the adolescents live. Beneficence refers to the obligation to minimize harm to the participant and advance the welfare of the participant and community. Justice demands that all individuals who may benefit from the research have an equal opportunity to participate and that no demographic group endures an unfair burden during the research process. SAM argues that adolescents who engage in substance abuse and other sensitive behaviors will not participate in research unless they are assured of confidentiality. Without the participation of these youths, important data about effective prevention and treatment interventions will not be accessed.

Cultural and Community Considerations

Disparities in the availability, accessibility, and quality of mental health services for minority populations represent a significant problem (DHHS 2001a). The elimination of disparities in mental health care can be achieved by conducting research to investigate the efficacy of ethnic- or culture-specific interventions for minority populations, translating that research into clinical settings and improving community outreach.

Several researchers (e.g., Fisher and Wallace 2000; Santelli et al. 2003) identified the importance of community consultation regarding socially sensitive research that involves or affects that community. It is essential for the specific community, especially if it comprises ethnic minority groups, to understand the purpose of the research. The community helps assess the study's potential benefit and harm to the individual participants and its social value to their community. This obligates researchers to understand that community's norms and values.

Conclusion

Clinical treatment and research with youths who abuse substances produce ethical uncertainties. Health care professionals are expected to grasp state and federal regulations that pertain to minors who seek confidential care for substance abuse, developmental issues related to childhood and adolescence, the empirical data that support treatment effectiveness, and their philosophy and values toward including or excluding the family from treatment. Researchers are also obligated to include underrepresented populations in their studies and to integrate the needs of the local communities into their research queries. Providers must be aware of their own values with regard to substance abuse in general and, more specifically, to youths who abuse substances and engage in other illegal or dishonest behaviors. All those who work with youths, especially youths who engage in high-risk behaviors, must approach the ethical crossroad with the capacity to negotiate the manifold demands of the youths, their families, their communities, and legal and professional standards; explore their own intentions and motivations; and consult with trusted colleagues.

Core Concepts

- Providers recognize the individual patient's dignity, autonomy, and capacity for self-determination. Mature minors are afforded the legal right to provide their own informed consent for substance abuse treatment. Providers must ascertain that the substance abuse has not impaired the mature minor's judgment.

- Providers always act in the best interest of the client. This may necessitate the involvement of the minor's family in treatment.

- Evidence-based treatments for substance abuse incorporate a developmental perspective and include cognitive-behavioral therapy and family-based interventions.

- The three guiding principles of research—autonomy, beneficence, and justice—apply to research with youths. Minors who live in states that allow them to consent to their own treatment may consent to participate in treatment research.

- Providers practice within the scope of their professional competence, comprehend normal and abnormal child development, appreciate the contextual world in which youths live, and appraise their own attitudes toward substance abuse.

Type up

Case Examples	Core Concepts
Steve, a sixteen-year-old adolescent, seeks treatment for substance abuse and does not want his parents to be involved in treatment.	Mature minor; informed consent; confidential treatment
Rhoda, a seventeen-year-old adolescent, is referred to a mental health professional for substance abuse treatment. The provider utilizes an interpersonal approach to treatment.	Practicing within scope of professional competence; evidence-based treatment interventions
Carol, a school professional, conducts research with a class of eighth graders to determine if psychoeducational interventions reduce substance abuse in middle school youth.	Autonomy, beneficence, justice; informed consent; assent of minors
Benjamin, a juvenile probation officer, wants a clinician to disclose details about an adolescent's substance abuse treatment.	Patient dignity, autonomy, and capacity for self-determination; confidentiality; informed consent

9

Ethical Dilemmas in Treating Chronic Pain in the Context of Addiction

JOANNA G. KATZMAN, M.D., M.S.P.H.

CYNTHIA M. A. GEPPERT, M.D., PH.D., M.P.H.

Chronic, nonmalignant pain is one of the major reasons adults seek medical care. Headache, back pain, and joint-related syndromes such as arthritis are the major causes of absenteeism within the American labor force. Back pain is also the leading cause of disability claims in the United States (Langworthy 1993; Portenoy and Cruciani 2007; Stewart et al. 2003).

Treating Chronic Nonmalignant Pain

There is increasing government and institutional recognition that pain treatment in many health care organizations has been neglected and is inadequate, causing unnecessary suffering, disability, depression, and prolonged rehabilitation. In 2001, the Joint Commission (then known as the Joint Commission on Accreditation of Healthcare Organizations or JCAHO) implemented pain treatment standards that hospitals must meet for accreditation. A Veterans Health Administration Directive issued in 2003 described the assessment of pain as the "fifth vital sign" to be evaluated when patients are seen by a medical provider (Veterans Health Administration 2003). Unlike blood pressure or temperature recordings, however, it remains difficult to objectively assess the severity of pain based on a simple "zero to ten" pain scale, because pain is always partly a subjective experience. Chronic pain, for example, involves not only physical symptoms but also psychological, emotional, behavioral, and social influences.

Intractable pain affects not only the patient but also the family members closely involved with caring for the patient and involves society as a whole through lost productivity and health care costs.

The most effective treatment of chronic, nonmalignant pain incorporates a multidisciplinary team approach (Golden 2002). A comprehensive pain management program or clinic incorporates pharmacological treatments, interventional treatments, psychiatric evaluation, behavioral medicine approaches, and rehabilitation. (See Table 9.1, Selected Therapies in a Multidisciplinary Pain Program for a list of therapies that relate to the different types of pain treatment.) Addiction therapists, substance abuse counselors, and other mental health professionals are often valuable members of these interdisciplinary teams that work with patients who have both chronic pain and psychiatric and addiction problems. It is thus important for addiction clinicians of all disciplines to have a general idea of the modern approach to pain treatment, particularly with narcotic medications, so they can assist patients in benefiting from chronic pain therapies without relapsing into use of substances or developing a new addiction. Historically, the pain and addiction communities have not collaborated or had clear and collegial understanding of each other's methods and goals. This has often led to confused patients and resulted in fragmented and inadequate patient care.

The pharmacological treatment of chronic pain incorporates many different medicine classifications. Analgesics are the most commonly used medications, especially for back pain and arthritis. It is important to note that opiates are only one type of analgesic preparation. Nonopiate analgesics such as acetaminophen or ibuprofen should always be tried first, unless contraindications or adverse effects are noted. Other classifications of medications for pain relief also depend upon the type of pain being treated. Neuropathic and radicular pain are treated with many types of antiepileptic drugs, as well as various antidepressants. Increased tone and muscle spasticity are treated with antispasticity medications. There are two main types of treatment for migraine

TABLE 9.1

Selected Therapies in a Multidisciplinary Pain Program

Types of Pain Treatment	Representative Examples
Medication	Analgesics, antiepileptics, antidepressants, muscle relaxants
Intervention	Trigger point injections, epidural steroid injections, nerve blocks
Psychology	Cognitive-behavioral therapy, biofeedback, hypnosis
Rehabilitation	Physical therapy, vocational rehabilitation, exercise
Prosthesis	Cane, walker, orthothesis

headaches. Abortive treatments stop acute headaches and include the family of triptans, ergotamines, and analgesics, both over the counter and by prescription. Prophylactic treatments prevent headaches and include calcium channel blockers, beta-blockers, and antiepileptic drugs.

Chronic Pain Treatment and Addiction

The area of pain treatment that has been the most controversial and detrimental is in the use of opioids as part of a harm reduction program for treating a patient's chronic pain in the context of addiction to alcohol or other drugs. Four primary concerns include (1) a lack of clarity and consensus regarding clinical indications for opioids in chronic rather than acute or terminal pain, (2) side effects and psychomotor impairments from opioid therapy that may interfere with rather than improve functioning,

(3) the risks of causing tolerance or addiction in patients, particularly those with substance use histories, and (4) realistic fears of diversion and other negative public health consequences. The treatment of chronic, nonmalignant pain, particularly with opioid medications, involves clinical, social, legal, and ethical issues because of its relationship to addiction. The risk that patients treated for chronic pain with narcotics will misuse or abuse prescription drugs, develop a new substance use disorder, or relapse to a previous problem complicates the treatment of painful medical conditions and often leaves clinicians facing ethical dilemmas. Substance use disorders and addiction rates have reached an all-time high in the United States. The 2005 National Survey on Drug Use and Health found that twenty-two million Americans over age twelve meet the criteria for abuse and dependence upon illicit drugs. This survey also notes that the population of persons using opiates for nonmedicinal purposes is estimated to be well over four million (Substance Abuse and Mental Health Services Administration 2006).

Due to these high rates of prescription opioid abuse and dependence, the treatment of chronic, nonmalignant pain with narcotics is a subject of debate and disagreement among the medical and legal community. There is today no question that the treatment of terminal cancer pain and other end-of-life illnesses with opiates is considered morally, legally, and ethically imperative. Additionally, there is growing consensus not only that it is acceptable but also that it is the standard of care to offer opiate analgesic medications to persons in need of more efficacious pain control for chronic, nonmalignant pain. It remains controversial, however, to treat chronic pain patients using opiates when such patients have a history of substance abuse or, even more, an active problem with addiction. Further complicating the ethical analysis is the fact that a large percentage of patients with substance use disorders have comorbid chronic pain. One recent study of 390 subjects from methadone maintenance treatment programs found that 37 percent of patients reported severe chronic pain symptoms in addition to their history of opiate addiction. Furthermore, 68 percent of these patients reported experiencing levels of pain that interfered with daily function (Rosenblum et al. 2003).

Pain and Addiction Terminology

Because the treatment of chronic, nonmalignant pain with opiate analgesics in a patient with a history of substance abuse disorders remains a controversial therapeutic option, it is important to understand some of the differences in widely used, and often misused, pain and addiction terminology. Tolerance to opiate analgesics is the state of adaptation to the drug, resulting in the reduction of the drug's effects over time. It has been thought to involve a down-regulation of the mu opiate receptor (Martin et al. 1999). Physical dependence is a drug-specific withdrawal phenomenon triggered by abrupt cessation of the drug, lowering the medication dose, or administering a drug-specific antagonist (naloxone). Unlike physical dependence to opiates, which is a well-described syndrome some persons experience when using chronic opiates for pain control, the problem of addiction is far less common. Addiction, by definition, is a primary, chronic, neurobiological disease, characterized by impaired control of use (escalating doses, early refills), compulsive use (for nonmedicinal purposes), continued use despite harm to oneself or others, and continued craving (Savage et al. 2001).

The signs and symptoms of addiction can closely resemble the behaviors seen in the patient who remains in severe pain and is undertreated, known as pseudoaddiction. Many patients who request early refills, escalate doses of opiates on their own, or frequent the emergency room may in fact be receiving inadequate pain treatment. It is often difficult to discern addiction from pseudoaddiction, but it is one of the most important behaviors for addiction professionals and pain specialists to understand. Patients with undertreatment of pain need close follow-up and monitoring to optimize their pain control. Unfortunately, too often uneducated or overwhelmed acute care providers label these patients as "addicts," resulting in termination of their prescriptions and a stigmatization that often adversely affects their medical care for decades.

One of the most important considerations, then, in caring for the patient on opiates with chronic, nonmalignant pain is careful documentation of aberrant behaviors and side effects from the medications, which most commonly include constipation, excessive sedation, and hyperalgesia. It is crucial to document pain relief obtained from opiates and improvement in function. Functional improvement refers to increasing mobility, the ability to perform activities of daily living independently, and returning to work. This documentation is considered ethically and legally imperative to justify the use of opiates for chronic, nonmalignant pain in all patients, with or without a substance abuse history.

The Ethical Dilemma of Treating Pain and Preventing Addiction

The frequent co-occurrence of chronic pain and substance use disorders generates two overlapping ethical dilemmas, which both patients and addiction professionals must navigate. First, it is essential to provide relief from suffering and to avoid undertreatment of pain. However, medical providers need to be aware of the potential for drug abuse and diversion. Hippocrates' dictum that physicians must "produce good for the patient and protect that patient from harm" defines the two poles of the dilemma.

On one hand is the reality of inadequate pain treatment in this country, particularly among the marginalized populations that also have a high comorbidity of substance use disorders. A 1996 study of 366 ambulatory AIDS patients found that 226 of them reported frequent pain in the two weeks prior to the survey. When the appropriateness of pain treatment was assessed using a standardized instrument, 85 percent of patients were receiving inadequate pain therapy, and fewer than 8 percent of the 110 patients in severe pain were prescribed an opioid indicated for this degree of pain in expert guidelines. Women, the less educated, and patients with a history of intravenous drug use were the most likely groups to have their pain inadequately controlled (Breitbart et al. 1996).

The risk of iatrogenic opiate addiction in the context of chronic pain therapy is also very real. Estimates in the literature indicate that 5 percent to 19 percent of patients receiving opioid therapy for chronic pain develop a substance use problem. Clinicians in preventive management can find assistance by studying the ongoing research that is now looking into the risk factors most closely associated with aberrant behavior. Recent studies have suggested that opiate addiction rates can remain low if chronic pain patients with a history of substance abuse are treated within the setting of a closely monitored, comprehensive pain management program (Ballantyne and Mao 2003). Careful patient selection, judicious use of opiate contracts, and regular office visits, along with the use of adjunctive medications and nonpharmacological treatments, can keep opiate addiction rates to a minimum (Ballantyne 2006).

Ethical Principles, Pain, and Addiction

The same core ethical principles and virtues that were important in providing clinical guidance in the previous chapters of this book can also assist providers in resolving the ethical dilemmas encountered in treating chronic pain in patients with substance use disorders. Compassion for those who suffer from both chronic pain and addiction is the primary virtue that addiction clinicians must cultivate to competently manage this challenging population. Other central ethical concepts and their application to pain and substance use disorders are summarized in Table 9.2, Ethical Principles in Pain and Addiction.

Pervasive social biases and cultural attitudes may make it difficult for addiction professionals to maintain their respect for clients who have abused pain medications or who have criminal justice involvement. All too frequently patients who display aberrant behavior, such as "losing their prescription," or relapse to other forms of substance use are discharged from treatment or

TABLE 9.2

Ethical Principles in Pain and Addiction

Principles	Application to Pain and Addiction
Respect for persons	Respect for the dignity of the individual no matter the behavior
Autonomy	Respecting the client's values and treatment preferences when these are consonant with clinical and ethical standards of care Obtaining informed consent for all therapies
Nonmaleficence	Balancing risks and benefits of opioid treatment for chronic pain to minimize harm to the patient
Beneficence	Focusing on function rather than relief of pain Emphasizing medical and not legal perspectives in clinical care
Justice	Understanding that both addiction and pain are chronic biopsychosocial diseases that are fundamentally no different from other medical conditions
Confidentiality	Safeguarding the higher standards applied to addiction treatment
Truth telling	Honest and full disclosure of information regarding pain and addiction

have their pain complaints dismissed as "drug seeking." Even when a practitioner must deny a patient's request for opioids or stop current narcotic therapy, the medications must be humanely tapered to avoid withdrawal, while nonaddictive interventions for pain and alternative effective addiction treatments are intensified.

Autonomy is the prevailing value in Western medical ethics, but it has some nuances and limitations when applied to addiction treatment. Pain and addiction can impair patients' thinking and valuation so that they may request therapies, such as opioids or benzodiazepines, that may not be in their best interest. In these situations, the addiction clinician can empathetically honor patients' wishes for relief from pain and anxiety only when these are consonant with the ethical priority of "do no harm" and clinical standards of care. When addiction clinicians conduct a deliberate and carefully documented informed consent discussion of risks, benefits, and alternatives for management of each disorder, they can often develop a treatment plan that balances patient preferences and provider obligations. Although opioid contracts are often utilized to structure treatment planning for patients who are identified as at risk for abusing opioids or who have displayed misuse of prescriptions, many ethicists see such contracts as more protective of the provider than the patient and as generating for clinicians conflicts of interest between legal or administrative considerations and therapeutic alliances (Rich 2005). A more constructive strategy is to emphasize beneficence in treating the patient who has both pain and substance use disorders, which might be understood as improving quality of life and functioning but not providing complete relief from pain. Similarly, practitioners who focus on recovery from addiction in all its dimensions with full recognition that it is a relapsing condition are operating from medical rather than legal motivations.

Chronicity and nonadherence are not unique to addiction or pain disorders but are aspects of almost all nonacute medical disorders, such as diabetes and asthma. Patients become physically dependent upon, tolerant to, and exhibit withdrawal from many noncontrolled substances, such as antihypertensives and antidepressants. The principle of justice requires that "equals should be treated equally and nonequals be treated not-equally," which means that persons with substance use disorders and chronic pain must not be discriminated against or denied appropriate care purely on the basis of physiological phenomena like withdrawal and dependence or psychological behaviors such as nonadherence to treatment regimens or relapse. It is precisely the likelihood of a greater degree of stigmatization that warrants the higher level of confidentiality protections afforded substance-abuse-related medical information. Addiction clinicians have an ethical duty to understand and observe the higher standards of privacy protection owed to their patients. Conversely, the potentially detrimental medical, social, and even legal consequences of substance use in the context of chronic pain must be fully and forthrightly explained to patients, and the patients' authentic and voluntary consent must be secured and documented.

A Harm Reduction Approach
The theory and practice of harm reduction is covered in Chapter 3, The Ethics of Harm Reduction.

Here it is discussed as one approach to reconciling the ethical dilemma inherent in treating the chronic pain of persons with past or current substance use disorders. Reasonable trust in patients' veracity and intentions until proven otherwise is a wise stance to adopt for any clinician engaged in treating patients suffering from chronic pain and addiction. The training of many addiction professionals, particularly those who are not physicians, likely taught them to regard the prescription of controlled substances to persons with substance use disorders as unwise and unwarranted, and some self-help groups may actually consider the use of such drugs, even for pain, as contradicting their recovery philosophies and as merely a legal form of self-medication. While respecting these viewpoints, it is important for clinicians of all disciplines to recognize that patients with substance use disorders often have a lower pain tolerance and higher pain medication threshold than their non-substance-using peers. As such, patients with a history of substance use may require more aggressive pain treatment than

TABLE 9.3

Ten Steps in the Ethical Management of Chronic Pain

Step 1: Establish the pathophysiology of pain where possible and appropriate.

Step 2: Begin with nonpharmacological treatments and move to medications only if these do not provide sufficient relief.

Step 3: Maximize use of non-narcotic adjunctive medications before utilizing opioids.

Step 4: Minimize risk of addiction by using long-acting opioid preparations and scheduled dosing rather than short-acting drugs on an as-needed basis.

Step 5: Employ a multimodal approach including physical therapy, Twelve Step work, acupuncture, family therapy, and vocational therapy for an integrative approach to the whole person.

Step 6: Keep in mind that patients with a history of addiction often require higher doses of opioids for adequate control of pain.

Step 7: Teach patients that there is no cure for addiction. It is a lifelong struggle with expected relapse and recovery.

Step 8: Help patients set realistic expectations and goals regarding benefits and side effects of medications: "not 'No pain,' but functional gain."

Step 9: Utilize objective pain ratings, addiction assessments, and quality of life measures to evaluate response.

Step 10: Judiciously employ opioid contracts and toxicology screens to prevent and monitor aberrant behavior within the context of a trusting provider-patient relationship.

Adapted from Geppert (2004)

a patient with no history of addiction. Although it may seem counterintuitive, patients with pain and substance use disorders may actually use substances of abuse, such as alcohol, less frequently or in lesser amounts if their pain is adequately controlled, because many patients use drugs and alcohol for analgesia (Alford, Compton, and Samet 2006). Without adequate pain treatment, some patients will use illicit opioids to control their pain, which increases their risk of contracting HIV, hepatitis C, and other infectious diseases.

Historically the separate education and clinical work of addiction and pain professionals has led to mutual misunderstandings, and this lack of collaboration has not served patients well. The improvement in outcomes of dual diagnosis patients treated in co-occurring disorders programs, as reviewed in Chapter 4, is mirrored when patients with pain and addiction are served in integrated settings. Currie and colleagues followed forty-four patients treated in such an integrated ten-week program for twelve months after discharge. They found no difference in patients who continued to take opioids for pain and those patients who were not currently taking narcotics, despite the fact that two-thirds of the patients were opioid dependent. Both groups showed comparable reduction in overall medication use and reduced pain, although those on opioids showed better overall functioning (Currie et al. 2003).

Another promising harm reduction option that involves the close collaboration of primary care physicians, addiction professionals, and pain specialists in the treatment of comorbid pain and addiction is the use of buprenorphine. This partial opioid agonist was approved in 2003 for the treatment of opioid dependence and is the first such therapy to be offered in a physician's office. One of the requirements for certification to prescribe buprenorphine is the ability to refer a patient to an addiction program or counselor, providing an ideal opportunity to engage the patient with pain and addiction in substance use treatment. Although buprenorphine is not FDA-approved for pain treatment, studies are rapidly demonstrating its potential for safely and simultaneously managing both pain and addiction (Kahan et al. 2006).

A final, and perhaps the most significant, component of harm reduction in which addiction professionals play a crucial role is the vigorous diagnosis and treatment of other comorbid mental health and psychosocial problems. The overlapping epidemiology of pain, addiction, and psychiatric disorders may manifest in use of opioids for psychoactive purposes, such as relief of anxiety or depression, fear of health care being revoked unless illness behavior is exhibited, or the idea that substances—including prescription medications—can substitute for the hard work of personal change. The same messages of individual responsibility, acceptance of relapse as an expected part of recovery, and the need to develop adaptive means of coping with the suffering, frustration, and disappointment endemic to the human condition are also the core of successful addiction treatment and are the essential lessons of effective pain management.

Conclusion

In 2004 the American Pain Society, the American Academy of Pain Medicine, and the American Society of Addiction Medicine released a landmark public policy statement on the rights and responsibilities of health care professionals when using opioids to treat pain: "Persistent failure to use opioids effectively when they are indicated as part of the treatment of pain, including in persons with active or recovering addiction, is poor medical practice and may also become grounds for practice concern" (Public policy statement 2004). Ethical resolution of the often conflicting clinical duties to maximize relief of pain while minimizing the harms of addiction may be the most challenging, but also the most rewarding, work clinicians in each field will confront in their professional careers.

Joanna G. Katzman, M.D., M.S.P.H. • Cynthia M. A. Geppert, M.D., Ph.D., M.P.H.

Core Concepts

- When treating chronic pain in patients with a history of substance use or addiction, a harm reduction approach, which emphasizes improvement in function and movement toward recovery, may be the most beneficial.

- Opioids may be one part of a multidisciplinary approach to chronic pain even for persons with a history of addiction.

- When treating patients with a history of substance use or addiction, the application of core ethical principles and values to pain and addiction treatment can assist in reconciling ethical dilemmas.

Read these ✓

next page ↗

Case Examples	Core Concepts
Jim, a fifty-eight-year-old Vietnam veteran, has chronic low back pain due to severe degenerative disc disease and facet arthropathy of his lumbar spine. Jim calls the pain clinic for an early refill of his oxycodone/acetaminophen medication because of escalating pain in his low back. His monthly refill of opiates is not due for one week. Jim has been a responsible and treatment-compliant patient at the comprehensive pain center for over five years, and his pain has been under good control with the use of opiate and non-opiate analgesic medications. Jim has exhibited improved function with his current medications and is now able to work part time. He also enjoys an improved quality of life. After discussing his request for an early refill, Jim tells the physician that he had been helping a friend move over the weekend and that he spent two days moving boxes and lifting heavy furniture.	A harm reduction approach, which emphasizes improvement in function and move-ment toward recovery, may be beneficial.
Lisa, a forty-four-year-old mother of two, has chronic neck pain. She presents to the pain management clinic with symptoms of opiate addiction and a desire for help with this problem. Lisa's current pain doctor has been prescribing her opiates for pain relief and has been slowly increasing the doses at any sign of increasing pain. Lisa states that she underwent a cervical fusion approximately four years ago for cervical disc bulges and neural foraminal narrowing of the exiting cervical nerve roots. This was causing severe radicular pain into both of her arms. After the surgery, Lisa was immediately placed on short- and long-acting oxy-codone for pain relief. No other non-opiate analgesics, other adjunctive medications, or rehabilitation were prescribed. Upon taking a detailed past medical and social history, the pain physician ascertains that Lisa had a significant heroin addiction ten years prior.	The need to relieve chronic pain and avoid triggering or worsening addiction creates an ethical dilemma.

Case Examples	Core Concepts
Matt, a twenty-six-year-old man, was recently discharged from a four-month stay at an inpatient substance abuse treatment center for cocaine and alcohol abuse. Matt has been cocaine and alcohol free for less than one year but remains in closely monitored outpatient treatment. Matt now presents to the pain management clinic for ongoing severe neuropathic pain in his legs and feet related to diabetic peripheral neuropathy. He has not responded to high doses of medications typically used as first line for this painful condition. He is requesting an opiate trial to relieve his pain. Matt submits to a urine tox screen and blood alcohol level at his pain clinic evaluation, and the results show no illicit substances, alcohol, or opiates.	*Opioids may be one part of a multidisciplinary approach to chronic pain even for persons with a history of addiction.*
Sara, a thirty-nine-year-old musician, has chronic intractable migraine headaches. She presents to the comprehensive pain management program asking for refills on her long-acting oxycodone, 100 mg three times per day. During the physician's initial evaluation, Sara states that her headaches are so severe that at times she has needed to find many doctors to fill her opiate medications. Sara states that if she runs out of medications, she buys them from acquaintances in her neighborhood or goes to the emergency room for pain relief. Sara has also admitted to using illicit substances at times to relieve her suffering. When Sara was asked to provide a urine toxicology screen as part of the initial evaluation, she never made it down to the laboratory to provide the sample.	*The application of the core ethical principles and values to pain and addiction treatment can assist in reconciling the dilemma.*

Cynthia M. A. Geppert, M.D., Ph.D., M.P.H.

Dr. Geppert is chief of consultation psychiatry and ethics at the New Mexico Veterans Affairs Health Care System, where she specializes in the care of patients with bipolar disorder, dual diagnosis, and trauma. She is an assistant professor in the Department of Psychiatry and director of ethics  education at the University of New Mexico School of Medicine, and the associate director of the Religious Studies Program at the University of New Mexico. She is an ordained priest in the Independent Catholic tradition. Dr. Geppert teaches, writes, and conducts research in consultation psychiatry, clinical ethics, spirituality, medical education, addiction, and psychopharmacology.

Laura Weiss Roberts, M.D., M.A.

Dr. Roberts serves as chairman and Charles E. Kubly Professor in the Department of Psychiatry and Behavioral Medicine at the Medical College of Wisconsin, Milwaukee, Wisconsin. An NIH-funded career scientist with a special populations focus, Dr. Roberts is a nationally recognized  scholar and leader in ethics, psychiatry, medicine, and medical education. She created a multidisciplinary research team, the Empirical Ethics Group, in 1996. A dedicated writer, she has written extensively on topics including professionalism, clinical and research ethics, informed consent, clinical medicine, rural health care, health disparities, educational scholarship, end-of-life care, and physician and medical student health care.

Jerald Belitz, Ph.D.

Dr. Belitz is associate professor and chief psychologist in the Department of Psychiatry and clinical director of the Children's Psychiatric Center/Outpatient Services, University of New Mexico Health Sciences Center, Albuquerque, New Mexico. He specializes in program development and community collaboration. He has worked in both inpatient and outpatient services and is actively involved in teaching and supervising trainees from various behavioral health disciplines. He co-teaches an interactive ethics seminar for child and adolescent psychiatry residents and psychology interns. He helped develop and implement a community-based wraparound model of care for youth and families with multiple psychosocial problems.

Michael P. Bogenschutz, M.D.

Dr. Bogenschutz is professor of psychiatry and vice-chair for addiction psychiatry, University of New Mexico Health Sciences Center and Center on Alcoholism, Substance Abuse, and Addictions, Albuquerque, New Mexico. He also directs the Addiction Psychiatry Fellowship program in the Department of Psychiatry. Dr. Bogenschutz heads a program of clinical research in addiction treatment, including federally funded studies of novel pharmacologic and behavioral therapies for drug and alcohol addiction and co-occurring disorders. He is principal investigator of the Southwest Node of the NIDA Clinical Trials Network and holds a K24 midcareer grant from NIAAA.

Diane T. Castillo, Ph.D.

Dr. Castillo is the coordinator of the Women's Stress Disorder Treatment Team within the Behavioral Health Care Line at the New Mexico Veterans Affairs Health Care System and professor in the psychiatry and psychology departments at the University of New Mexico. She is active in conducting research in PTSD and has administered two national cooperative research projects on assessment and treatment of PTSD. Other research and publications have been in the area of cross-cultural treatment of Hispanic veterans with PTSD and treatment of anger in a VA population.

Christie A. Cline, M.D., M.B.A.

Dr. Cline is founder and president of ZiaLogic in Albuquerque, New Mexico, and ZiaPartners in San Rafael, California, providing consultation, products, and technical assistance nationally and internationally to behavioral health care systems in policy, procedure, and practices for integrated services development, quality improvement, and systems transformation. She is a leading expert on the implementation of the Comprehensive Continuous Integrated Systems of Care (CCISC) model in adult and child and adolescent systems of care and has worked in all types of systems and service settings with extraordinarily diverse populations, ranging from rural areas with significant Native American populations (e.g., New Mexico, Alaska, and Montana) to complex urban areas with severely impoverished inner-city populations (e.g., District of Columbia, Miami, and San Francisco), as well as areas, like Vancouver Island, British Columbia, that have North America's most highly diverse foreign-born populations. Dr. Cline developed the design and format of the CCISC Change Agent Approach and the Curriculum and has been largely responsible for linking the content of training to the overall quality improvement process for systems development. She is a coauthor of the CCISC Co-occurring Disorders Capability Toolkit and has published several articles on co-occurring disorder system development. Recognized as a national leader in the area of systems integration, she was a member of the SAMHSA consensus panel for development of TIP 42. As well, Dr. Cline was appointed to be on the SAMHSA national expert panel for the Co-occurring State Infrastructure Grant (COSIG) cross-site evaluation in 2007.

Alyssa A. Forcehimes, Ph.D.

Dr. Forcehimes is a postdoctoral fellow in clinical psychology at the University of New Mexico's Center on Alcoholism, Substance Abuse, and Addictions. Her primary research interest is addiction, focusing on its interface with spirituality. Currently, Dr. Forcehimes is the Southwest Node Coordinator for NIDA's Clinical Trials Network. She has published in the areas of motivational interviewing, Alcoholics Anonymous, and how changes in spirituality affect and are affected by substance use. Dr. Forcehimes is a member of the motivational interviewing network of trainers.

Joanna G. Katzman, M.D., M.S.P.H.

Dr. Katzman is assistant professor in neurology at the University of New Mexico. She is fellowship trained in neurorehabilitation. Dr. Katzman is currently the medical director of the Clinical Neurosciences Center and dedicates her neurology practice to headaches and chronic pain. She was formally the medical director of the Chronic Pain Program at the New Mexico Veterans Administration Health Care System. Dr. Katzman spends much time seeing patients in her practice as well as teaching pain management fellows, residents, and medical students.

Joseph B. Layde, M.D., J.D.

Dr. Layde is associate professor and vice-chair for education in the Department of Psychiatry and Behavioral Medicine at the Medical College of Wisconsin, Milwaukee, Wisconsin, where he also directs the Forensic Psychiatry Fellowship and teaches classes on bioethics for medical students and bioethics and the law for graduate students.

Jennifer Knapp Manuel, M.S.

Ms. Knapp Manuel is a doctoral candidate in clinical psychology at the University of New Mexico. Her research focuses on the involvement of family members in addiction treatment, as well as therapeutic processes in therapy sessions. She is a member of the Motivational Interviewing Network of Trainers (MINT) and is interested in training clinicians in empirically supported treatments. She currently works at the Center on Alcoholism, Substance Abuse, and Addictions, Albuquerque, New Mexico.

William R. Miller, Ph.D.

Dr. Miller is emeritus distinguished professor of psychology and psychiatry at the University of New Mexico. He served as director of clinical training for UNM's APA-approved doctoral program in clinical psychology and as codirector of UNM's Center on Alcoholism, Substance Abuse, and Addictions (CASAA). Dr. Miller's publications include forty books and more than four hundred articles and chapters. Fundamentally interested in the psychology of change, he has focused in particular on the development, testing, and dissemination of behavioral treatments for addictions. He served as principal investigator for numerous research grants and contracts, founded a private practice group, and served as a consultant to many organizations, including the U.S. Senate, the World Health Organization, the National Academy of Sciences, and the National Institutes of Health. In recognition of his research contributions, Dr. Miller is a recipient of the international Jellinek Memorial Award, two career achievement awards from the American Psychological Association, and an Innovators in Combating Substance Abuse award from the Robert Wood Johnson Foundation. He maintains an active interest in pastoral counseling and the integration of spirituality and psychology.

Kenneth Minkoff, M.D.

Dr. Minkoff is a board-certified, dedicated community psychiatrist with a certificate of additional qualifications in addiction psychiatry. He is a clinical assistant professor of psychiatry at Harvard Medical School and a senior systems consultant for ZiaPartners in San Rafael, California. He is recognized as one of the nation's leading experts on integrated treatment of individuals with co-occurring psychiatric and substance disorders and on the development of integrated systems of care for such individuals, through the implementation of a national consensus best practice model for systems design: the Comprehensive Continuous Integrated System of Care (CCISC), referenced in SAMHSA's Report to Congress on Co-occurring Disorders (2002). Dr. Minkoff's major professional activity is training and consultation on clinical services and systems design for individuals and families with mental health and substance use disorders. With his consulting partner Dr. Cline, Dr. Minkoff has developed a systems change toolkit for CCISC implementation.

Kamilla L. Venner, Ph.D.

Dr. Venner is a visiting and research assistant professor in the Department of Psychology at the University of New Mexico and the Center on Alcoholism, Substance Abuse, and Addictions. She is an Alaska Native clinical psychologist and has led two NIH-funded research grants on improving substance abuse treatments for Native Americans. Dr. Venner is a member of the MINT network of motivational interviewing (MI) trainers and has written a manual to guide the practice of MI with Native American clients. She also focuses on training providers serving Native Americans. She has published in the areas of addiction, recovery, cross-cultural applicability, and adapting empirically supported interventions cross-culturally.

V. Ann Waldorf, Ph.D.

Dr. Waldorf is the chief of psychology and associate director of the Behavioral Health Care Line at New Mexico Veterans Affairs Health Care System, Albuquerque, New Mexico. Particular interests include substance use disorders, especially in individuals with comorbid psychiatric diagnoses, as well as the role of spiritual and religious beliefs in psychotherapy.

Chapter 1

Appelbaum, P. S. 2002. Privacy in psychiatric treatment: Threats and responses. *American Journal of Psychiatry* 159 (11): 1809–18.

Bogenschutz, M. P. 2004. Caring for persons with addictions. In *Concise guide to ethics in mental health care,* ed. L. W. Roberts and A. R. Dyer. Washington, D.C.: American Psychiatric Publishing.

Brooks, M. K. 2005. Legal aspects of confidentiality and patient information. In *Substance abuse: A comprehensive textbook,* ed. J. H. Lowinson, P. Ruiz, R. B. Millman, and J. G. Langrod, 1361–82. 4th ed. Philadelphia: Lippincott Williams & Wilkins.

Caplan, A. L. 2006. Ethical issues surrounding forced, mandated, or coerced treatment. *Journal of Substance Abuse Treatment* 31 (2): 117–20.

Carrese, J. A., and L. A. Rhodes. 1995. Western bioethics on the Navajo reservation: Benefit or harm? *JAMA* 274 (10): 826–29.

Center for Substance Abuse Treatment. 1994. *Intensive outpatient treatment for alcohol and drug abuse.* Washington, D.C.: U.S. Government Printing Office.

Centers for Disease Control and Prevention. 2004. Alcohol-attributable deaths and years of potential life lost—United States, 2001. *Morbidity and Mortality Weekly Report,* 53 (37): 866–70.

Cheng, T. L., J. A. Savageau, A. L. Sattler, and T. G. DeWitt. 1993. Confidentiality in health care: A survey of knowledge, perceptions, and attitudes among high school students [see comments]. *JAMA* 269 (11): 1404–7.

Clark, W. H., and M. K. Brooks. 2003. Ethical issues in addiction treatment. In *Principles of addiction medicine,* ed. A. W. Graham, T. K. Schultz, M. F. May-Smith, R. K. Ries, and B. B. Wilford. 3rd ed. Chevy Chase, Md.: American Society of Addiction Medicine.

Dwyer, J., and A. Shih. 1998. The ethics of tailoring the patient's chart [see comments]. *Psychiatric Services* 49 (10): 1309–12.

Felthous, A. R. 1993. Substance abuse and the duty to protect. *Bulletin of the American Academy of Psychiatry and the Law* 21 (4): 419–26.

Jonsen, A. R., M. Siegler, and W. J. Winslade. 1998. *Clinical ethics.* 4th ed. New York: McGraw-Hill.

Kessler, R. C., P. Berglund, O. Demler, R. Jin, K. R. Merikangas, and E. E. Walters. 2005. Lifetime prevalence and age-of-onset distributions of DSM-IV disorders in the National Comorbidity Survey Replication. *Archives of General Psychiatry* 62 (6): 593–602.

Lewin Group. 2004. *The economic costs of drug abuse in the United States, 1992–2002.* No. 207303. Washington, D.C.: Executive Office of the President, Office of National Drug Control Policy.

Lloyd, G. E. R., ed. 1983. *Hippocratic writings.* London: Penguin Books.

Luoma, J. B., M. P. Twohig, T. Waltz, S. C. Hayes, N. Roget, M. Padilla et al. 2006. An investigation of stigma in individuals receiving treatment for substance abuse. *Addictive Behaviors* 32 (7): 1331–46.

Marlowe, D. B., K. C. Kirby, L. M. Bonieskie, D. J. Glass, L. D. Dodds, S. D. Husband et al. 1996. Assessment of coercive and noncoercive pressures to enter drug abuse treatment. *Drug and Alcohol Dependence* 42 (2): 77–84.

McGinnis, J. M., and W. H. Foege. 1999. Mortality and morbidity attributable to use of addictive substances in the United States. *Proceedings of the Association of American Physicians* 111 (2): 109–18.

McLellan, A. T., D. C. Lewis, C. P. O'Brien, and H. D. Kleber. 2000. Drug dependence, a chronic medical illness: Implications for treatment, insurance, and outcomes evaluation. *JAMA* 284 (13): 1689–95.

Miller, N. S., L. M. Sheppard, C. C. Colenda, and J. Magen. 2001. Why physicians are unprepared to treat patients who have alcohol- and drug-related disorders. *Academic Medicine* 76 (5): 410–18.

Rawson, R. A., A. Huber, M. McCann, S. Shoptaw, D. Farabee, C. Reiber et al. 2002. A comparison of contingency management and cognitive-behavioral approaches during methadone maintenance treatment for cocaine dependence. *Archives of General Psychiatry* 59 (9): 817–24.

Roberts, L. W., and L. B. Dunn. 2003. Ethical considerations in caring for women with substance use disorders. *Obstetrics and Gynecology Clinics of North America* 30 (3): 559–82.

Roberts, L. W., and A. R. Dyer, eds. 2004. Health care ethics committees in *Concise guide to ethics in mental health care.* Washington, D.C.: American Psychiatric Publishing.

Roberts, L. W., T. D. Warner, C. Lyketsos, E. Frank, L. Ganzini, and D. Carter. 2001. Perceptions of academic vulnerability associated with personal illness: A study of 1,027 students at nine medical schools. Collaborative Research Group on Medical Student Health. *Comprehensive Psychiatry* 42 (1): 1–15.

Room, R. 2006. Taking account of cultural and societal influences on substance use diagnoses and criteria. *Addiction* 101 (1): S31–S39.

Stone, D. B. 2000. *Alcohol and other drugs.* Rockville, Md.: Substance Abuse and Mental Health Services Administration.

Substance Abuse and Mental Health Services Administration. 2006. *Results from the 2005 National Survey on Drug Use and Health: National findings.* Rockville, Md.: Department of Health and Human Services.

———. 2007a. *2006 National Survey on Drug Use and Health.* Rockville, Md.: Office of Applied Studies.

———. 2007b. Drug Abuse Warning Network, 2005: National estimates of drug-related emergency department visits. http://www.oas.samhsa.gov/DAWN/2k5ed.cfm.

U.S. Department of Health and Human Services. 1994. *Intensive outpatient treatment for alcohol and other drug abuse.* Treatment Improvement Protocol 8. Rockville, Md.: Substance Abuse and Mental Health Services Administration.

Vuchinich, R. E., and C. A. Simpson. 1998. Hyperbolic temporal discounting in social drinkers and problem drinkers. *Experimental and Clinical Psychopharmacology* 6 (3): 292–305.

Walker, R., T. K. Logan, J. J. Clark, and C. Leukefeld. 2005. Informed consent to undergo treatment for substance abuse: A recommended approach. *Journal of Substance Abuse Treatment* 29 (4): 241–51.

Weiss, F. 2005. Neurobiology of craving, conditioned reward and relapse. *Current Opinion in Pharmacology* 5 (1): 9–19.

Chapter 2

American Psychological Association. 2002. Ethical principles of psychologists and code of conduct. *American Psychologist* 57:1060–73.

Barnett, J. E. Must some boundaries be crossed? *American Psychological Association Division 42 News and Views.* http://www.division42.org/MembersArea/Nws_Views/art icles/Ethics/boundaries.html. Retrieved June 7, 2007.

Bovee, C. N. 1998. Multiple role relationships and conflicts of interest. In *Ethics in psychology,* ed. G. P. Koocher and P. Keith-Spiegel. New York: Oxford University Press.

Chapman, C. 1997. Dual relationships in substance abuse treatment: Ethical implications. *Alcoholism Treatment Quarterly* 15 (2): 73–79.

Crits-Cristoph, P., K. Baranackie, J. S. Kurcias, A. T. Beck, K. Carroll, K. Perry, L. Luborsky, A. T. McLellan, G. E. Woody, L. Thompson, D. Gallagher, and C. Zitrin. 1991. Meta-analysis of therapist effects in psychotherapy outcome studies. *Psychotherapy Research* 2:81–91.

Culbreth, J. R., and L. D. Borders. 1998. Perceptions of the supervisory relationship: A preliminary qualitative study of recovering and nonrecovering substance abuse counselors. *Journal of Substance Abuse Treatment* 15 (4): 345–52.

Dilts, S. L., C. A. Clark, and R. J. Harmon. 1997. Self-disclosure and the treatment of substance abuse. *Journal of Substance Abuse Treatment* 14 (1): 67–70.

Doyle, K. 1997. Substance abuse counselors in recovery: Implications for the ethical issue of dual relationships. *Journal of Counseling and Development* 5:428–32.

Gibson, W. T., and K. S. Pope. 1993. The ethics of counseling: A national survey of certified counselors. *Journal of Counseling and Development* 71:330–36.

Hollander, J. K., S. Bauer, B. Herlihy, and V. McCollum. 2006. Beliefs of board certified substance abuse counselors regarding multiple relationships. *Journal of Mental Health Counseling* 28 (1): 84–94.

Miller, W. R., R. Benefield, and J. S. Tonigan. 1993. Enhancing motivation for change in problem drinking: A controlled comparison of two therapist styles. *Journal of Consulting and Clinical Psychology* 61 (3): 455–61.

Miller, W., and F. Miller. 1998. Mandated addiction services: Potential ethical dilemmas. In *Practicing in the new mental health marketplace: Ethical, legal, and moral issues,* ed. R. F. Small and L. R. Barnhill. Washington, D.C.: American Psychological Association.

Miller, W. R., and S. Rollnick. 2002. *Motivational interviewing: Preparing people for change.* 2nd ed. New York: Guilford Press.

Miller, W. R., C. A. Taylor, and J. C. West. 1980. Focused versus broad-spectrum behavior therapy for problem drinkers. *Journal of Consulting and Clinical Psychology* 48 (5): 590–601.

NAADAC Education and Research Foundation. 1995. *Income and compensation study of alcohol and drug counseling professionals.* Arlington, Va.: NAADAC.

Nielsen, L. A. 1988. Substance abuse, shame and professional boundaries and ethics: Disentangling the issues. *Alcoholism Treatment Quarterly* 4 (3): 109–37.

Norcross, J. C., and C. E. Hill. 2005. Compendium of empirically supported therapy relationships. In *Psychologists' desk reference,* ed. G. P. Koocher, J. C. Norcross, and S. S. Hill. 2nd ed. New York: Oxford University Press.

Pope, K. S., and V. A. Vetter. 1992. Ethical dilemmas encountered by members of the American Psychological Association: A national survey. *American Psychologist* 47 (3): 397–411.

Rogers, C. 1959. A theory of therapy, personality and interpersonal relationships as developed in the client-centered framework. In *Psychology: The study of a science,* ed. S. Koch. Vol. 3, *Formulations of the personal and social contexts,* 184–256. New York: McGraw-Hill.

Simpson, D. D., G. W. Joe, G. A. Rowan-Szal, and J. M. Greener. 1997. Drug abuse treatment process components that improve retention. *Journal of Substance Abuse Treatment* 14 (6): 565–72.

St. Germaine, J. 1996. Dual relationships and certified alcohol and drug counselors: A national study of ethical beliefs and behaviors. *Alcoholism Treatment Quarterly* 14 (2): 29–44.

Tarasoff v. Board of Regents of the University of California, 118 Cal. Rptr. 129, 529 P.2d 553 (1974); P. 2d 334 (Cal. Sup. Ct. 1976).

Volkow, N. D. 2003. The dual challenge of substance abuse and mental disorders. *NIDA Notes* 18 (5). http://www.nida.nih.gov/NIDA_notes/NNvol18N5/DirRepVol18N5.html. Retrieved March 25, 2007.

Chapter 3

Alden, L. 1978. Evaluation of a preventive self-management programme for problem drinkers. *Canadian Journal of Behavioural Science* 10:258–63.

Anton, R. F., S. S. O'Malley, D. A. Ciraulo, D. Couper, D. M. Donovan, D. R. Gastfriend et al. 2006. Combined pharmacotherapies and behavioral interventions for alcohol dependence: The COMBINE study; A randomized controlled trial. *JAMA* 295:2003–17.

Apodaca, T. R., and W. R. Miller. 2003. A meta-analysis of the effectiveness of bibliotherapy for alcohol problems. *Journal of Clinical Psychology* 59:289–304.

Armor, D. J., J. M. Polich, and H. B. Stambul. 1978. *Alcoholism and treatment.* New York: Wiley.

Brehm, S. S., and J. W. Brehm. 1981. *Psychological reactance: A theory of freedom and control.* New York: Academic Press.

Brown, R. A. 1980. Conventional education and controlled drinking education courses with convicted drunken drivers. *Behavior Therapy* 11:632–42.

Davies, D. L. 1962. Normal drinking by recovered alcohol addicts. *Quarterly Journal of Studies on Alcohol* 23:94–104.

Deci, E. L., and R. M. Ryan. 1985. *Intrinsic motivation and self-determination in human behavior.* New York: Plenum Press.

Frankl, V. E. 1963. *Man's search for meaning.* Boston: Beacon Press.

Graber, R. A., and W. R. Miller. 1988. Abstinence or controlled drinking goals for problem drinkers: A randomized clinical trial. *Psychology of Addictive Behaviors* 2:20–33.

Hester, R. K. 2003. Behavioral self-control training. In *Handbook of alcoholism treatment approaches: Effective alternatives,* ed. R. K. Hester and W. R. Miller, 152–64. 3rd ed. Boston: Allyn & Bacon.

Hester, R. K., and H. D. Delaney. 1997. Behavioral self-control program for Windows: Results of a controlled clinical trial. *Journal of Consulting and Clinical Psychology* 65:686–93.

Institute of Medicine. 1990. *Broadening the base of treatment for alcohol problems.* Washington, D.C.: National Academy Press.

Lovibond, S. H., and G. R. Caddy. 1970. Discriminated aversive control in the moderation of alcoholics' drinking behavior. *Behavior Therapy* 1:437–44.

Lozano, B. E., R. S. Stephens, and R. A. Roffman. 2006. Abstinence and moderate use goals in the treatment of marijuana dependence. *Addiction* 101:1589–97.

Meyers, R. J., and B. L. Wolfe. 2004. *Get your loved one sober: Alternatives to nagging, pleading, and threatening.* Center City, Minn.: Hazelden.

Miller, W. R., and L. M. Baca. 1983. Two-year follow-up of bibliotherapy and therapist-directed controlled drinking training for problem drinkers. *Behavior Therapy* 14:441–48.

Miller, W. R., L. A. Leckman, H. D. Delaney, and M. Tinkcom. 1992. Long-term follow-up of behavioral self-control training. *Journal of Studies on Alcohol* 53:249–61.

Miller, W. R., and R. F. Muñoz. 2005. *Controlling your drinking: Tools to make moderation work for you.* New York: Guilford Press.

Miller, W. R., and A. Page. 1991. Warm turkey: Other routes to abstinence. *Journal of Substance Abuse Treatment* 8:227–32.

Miller, W. R., A. Zweben, C. C. DiClemente, and R. C. Rychtarik. 1992. *Motivational Enhancement Therapy manual: A clinical research guide for therapists treating individuals with alcohol abuse and dependence.* Project MATCH Monograph Series 2. Rockville, Md.: National Institute on Alcohol Abuse and Alcoholism.

Mooney, C. 2005. *The Republican war on science.* New York: Basic Books.

Moyer, A., J. W. Finney, D. W. Swearingen, and P. Vergun. 2002. Brief interventions for alcohol problems: A meta-analytic review of controlled investigations in treatment-seeking and non-treatment-seeking populations. *Addiction* 97:279–92.

NIAAA (National Institute on Alcohol Abuse and Alcoholism). 1996 [May 28, 2001]. How to cut down on your drinking. http://pubs.niaaa.nih.gov/publications/handout.htm.

———. 2005. *Helping patients who drink too much: A clinician's guide.* Bethesda, Md.: NIAAA.

Pomerleau, O., M. Pertschuk, D. Adkins, and J. P. Brady. 1978. A comparison of behavioral and traditional treatment for middle-income problem drinkers. *Journal of Behavioral Medicine* 2:187–200.

Project MATCH Research Group. 1993. Project MATCH: Rationale and methods for a multisite clinical trial matching patients to alcoholism treatment. *Alcoholism: Clinical and Experimental Research* 17:1130–45.

———. 1997. Matching alcoholism treatments to client heterogeneity: Project MATCH posttreatment drinking outcomes. *Journal of Studies on Alcohol* 58:7–29.

Robertson, I., N. Heather, A. Dzialdowski, J. Crawford, and M. Winton. 1986. A comparison of minimal versus intensive controlled drinking treatment for problem drinkers. *British Journal of Clinical Psychology* 25:185–94.

Rychtarik, R. C., D. W. Foy, T. Scott, L. Lokey, and D. Prue. 1987. Five-six-year follow-up of broad-spectrum behavioral treatment for alcoholism: Effects of training controlled drinking skills. *Journal of Consulting and Clinical Psychology* 55:106–8.

Sanchez-Craig, M. 1980. Random assignment to abstinence or controlled drinking in a cognitive-behavioral program: Short-term effects on drinking behavior. *Addictive Behavior* 5:35–39.

Tiebout, H. M., L. Williams, M. L. Selzer, M. A. Block, R. Fox, I. Zwerling et al. 1963. Normal drinking in recovered alcohol addicts: Comments on the article by D. L. Davies. *Quarterly Journal of Studies on Alcohol* 24:321–32.

Vogler, R. E., J. V. Compton, and T. A. Weissbach. 1975. Integrated behavior change techniques for alcoholism. *Journal of Consulting and Clinical Psychology* 42:233–43.

Chapter 4

Center for Mental Health Services, Managed Care Initiative Panel on Co-occurring Disorders, K. Minkoff, chair. 1998. *Co-occurring psychiatric and substance disorders in managed care systems: Standards of care, practice guidelines, workforce competencies, and training curricula.* Philadelphia: Center for Mental Health Policy and Services Research.

Center for Substance Abuse Treatment. 2005. *Substance abuse treatment for individuals with co-occurring disorders.* Treatment Improvement Protocol 42. Rockville, Md.: Substance Abuse and Mental Health Services Administration.

Cline, C., and K. Minkoff. 2002. A strength-based systems approach to creating integrated services for individuals with co-occurring psychiatric and substance abuse disorders. SAMHSA Technical Assistance Document. New Mexico Department of Health (NMDOH)/BHSD, http://tie.samhsa.gov/topics/WORD/co-ocnewmexico final.doc.

Curie, C., K. Minkoff, G. Hutchins, and C. Cline. 2005. Strategic implementation of systems change for individuals with mental health and substance use disorders. *Journal of Dual Diagnosis* 1 (4): 75–95.

Daley, D., and H. Moss. 2002. *Dual disorders: Counseling clients with chemical dependency and mental illness.* 3rd ed. Center City, Minn.: Hazelden.

Drake, R. E., S. M. Essock et al. 2001. Implementing dual diagnosis services for clients with severe mental illness. *Psychiatric Services* 52 (4): 469–76.

Drake, R. E., A. I. Green, K. T. Mueser, and H. H. Goldman. 2003. The history of community mental health treatment and rehabilitation for persons with severe mental illness. *Community Mental Health Journal* 39 (5): 427–40.

Drake, R. E., G. J. McHugo, and D. L. Noordsy. 1993. Treatment of alcoholism among schizophrenic outpatients: Four-year outcomes. *American Journal of Psychiatry* 150 (2): 328–30.

Geppert, C. M. A., and K. Minkoff. 2003. *Psychiatric disorders and medications: A reference guide for professionals and their substance-dependent clients.* Center City, Minn.: Hazelden.

McHugo, G. J., R. E. Drake, H. L. Burton, and T. H. Ackerson. 1995. A scale for assessing the stage of substance abuse treatment in persons with severe mental illness. *Journal of Nervous and Mental Disorders* 183 (12): 762–67.

Miller, W. R., and S. Rollnick. 2002. *Motivational interviewing.* New York: Guilford Press.

Minkoff, K. 1991. Program components of a comprehensive integrated care system for serious mentally ill patients with substance disorders. In *Dual diagnosis of major mental illness and substance disorder,* ed. K. Minkoff and R. E. Drake, 13–27. New Directions for Mental Health Services, no. 50. San Francisco: Jossey-Bass.

Minkoff, K., and C. Cline. 2001. *CCISC Toolkit* CODECAT (Version 1): Co-occurring disorders educational competency assessment tool/Clinician core competencies for co-occurring psychiatric and substance abuse disorders. Albuquerque, N.M.: ZiaLogic.

———. 2004. Changing the world: The design and implementation of comprehensive continuous integrated systems of care for individuals with co-occurring disorders. *Psychiatric Clinics of North America* 27:727–43.

———. 2005. Developing welcoming systems for individuals with co-occurring disorders: The role of the comprehensive continuous integrated system of care model. *Journal of Dual Diagnosis* 1 (1): 39–64.

———. 2006. Dual diagnosis capability: Moving from concept to implementation. *Journal of Dual Diagnosis* 2 (2): 121–34.

Mueser, K. T., D. L. Noordsy, R. E. Drake, and L. Fox. 2003. *Integrated treatment for dual disorders: A guide to effective practice.* New York: Guilford Press.

Najavits, L., 2002. *Seeking safety: A treatment manual for PTSD and substance abuse.* New York: Guilford Press.

National Association of State Mental Health Program Directors/National Association of State Alcohol and Drug Abuse Directors. 1998. *The new conceptual framework for co-occurring mental health and substance use disorders.* Washington, D.C.: NASMHPD/NASADAD.

Prochaska, J. O., C. C. DiClemente, and J. C. Norcross. 1992. In search of how people change: Applications to addictive behaviors. *American Psychologist* 47:1102–14.

Roberts, L. J., A. Shaner, and T. A. Eckman. 1999. *Overcoming addictions: Skills training for people with schizophrenia.* New York: Norton.

Shaner, A. , and L. J. Roberts et al. 1997. Monetary reinforcement of abstinence from cocaine among mentally ill persons with cocaine dependence. *Psychiatric Services* 48:807–10.

Substance Abuse and Mental Health Services Administration (SAMHSA). 2002a. Report to Congress on the prevention and treatment of co-occurring substance abuse disorders and mental health disorders. http://www.samhsa.gov/reports/congress2002/index.html.

———. 2002b. *Results from the 2001 National Household Survey on Drug Abuse. Vol. 1, Summary of national findings.* DHHS Publication No. SMA 02-3758. Rockville, Md.: SAMHSA, Office of Applied Studies.

———. Center for Mental Health Services. In press. Integrated dual disorders treatment toolkit. Available at http://mental health.samhsa.gov/cmhs/communitysupport/toolkits/cooccurring/.

U. S. Department of Health and Human Services. Substance Abuse and Mental Health Services Administration, Center for Mental Health Services, National Institutes of Health, National Institute of Mental Health. 1999. Mental health: A report of the Surgeon General. http://www.surgeon general.gov/library/mentalhealth/home.html.

Ziedonis, D., and K. Trudeau. 1997. Motivation to quit using substances among individuals with schizophrenia: Implications for a motivation-based treatment model. *Schizophrenia Bulletin* 23:229–38.

Chapter 5

American Psychiatric Association. 2006. *The principles of medical ethics with annotations especially applicable to psychiatry.* Arlington, Va.: American Psychiatric Association.

American Psychological Association. 1993. Guidelines for providers of psychological services to ethnic, linguistic, and culturally diverse populations. *American Psychologist* 48:45–48.

———. 2003. Guidelines on multicultural education, training, research, practice, and organizational change for psychologists. *American Psychologist* 58:377–402.

Bishop, B. J., D. Higgins, F. Casella, and N. Contos. 2002. Reflections on practice: Ethics, race and worldviews. *Journal of Community Psychology* 30:611–21.

Duran, E., and B. Duran. 1995. *Native American postcolonial psychology.* New York: State University of New York Press.

Fadiman, A. 1997. *The spirit catches you and you fall down: A Hmong child, her American doctors, and the collision of two cultures.* New York: Farrar, Straus & Giroux.

Fowers, B. J., and B. J. Davidov. 2006. The virtue of multi-culturalism. *American Psychologist* 61:581–94.

Geppert, C. M. A., M. P. Bogenschutz, and W. R. Miller. 2007. Development of a bibliography on religion, spirituality and addictions. *Drug and Alcohol Review* 26 (4): 389–95.

Hansen, N. D., F. Pepitone-Arreola-Rockwell, and A. F. Greene. 2000. Multicultural competence: Criteria and case examples. *Professional Psychology: Research and Practice* 31:652–60.

Harper, M. G. 2006. Ethical multiculturalism: An evolutionary concept analysis. *Advances in Nursing Science* 29:110–24.

Kleinman, A. 1988. *The illness narratives: Suffering, healing, and the human condition.* New York: Basic Books.

Kleinman, A., and P. Benson. 2006. Anthropology in the clinic: The problem of cultural competency and how to fix it. *PloS Medicine* 3:e294.

La Marr, J., and G. A. Marlatt. 2007. *Canoe journey, life's journey.* Center City, Minn.: Hazelden.

Leino-Kilpi, H., M. Valilmaki, T. Dassen, M. Gasull, C. Lemonidou, P. A. Scott, A. Schopp, M. Arndt, and A. Kaljonen. 2003. Perceptions of autonomy, privacy, and informed consent in the care of elderly people in five European countries: Comparison and implications for the future. *Nursing Ethics* 10:58–66.

May, P. A. 1994. The epidemiology of alcohol abuse among American Indians: The mythical and real properties. *American Indian Culture and Research Journal* 18:121–43.

Meer, D., and L. VandeCreek. 2002. Cultural considerations in release of information. *Ethics and Behavior* 12:143–56.

Miller, W. R., and M. P. Bogenschutz. 2007. Spirituality and addiction. *Southern Medical Journal* 100 (4): 433–36.

NIAAA (National Institute on Alcohol Abuse and Alcoholism). 2004/2005. The scope of the problem. In *Alcohol and development in youth: A multidisciplinary overview.* Special issue, *Alcohol Research and Health* 28:111–20.

Room, R., A. Janca, L. A. Bennett, L. Schmidt, and N. Sartorius. 1996. WHO cross-cultural applicability research on diagnosis and assessment of substance use disorders: An overview of methods and selected results. *Addiction* 91:199–220.

Spicer, P., J. Beals, C. D. Croy, C. M. Mitchell, D. K. Novins, L. Moore, S. M. Manson, and the AISUPERPFP team. 2003. The prevalence of DSM-III-R alcohol dependence in two American Indian populations. *Alcoholism: Clinical and Experimental Research* 27:1785–97.

Sue, D. W., P. Arredondo, and R. J. McDavis. 1992. Multicultural counseling competencies and standards: A call to the profession. *Journal of Counseling and Development* 70:477–86.

Szapocznik, J., O. Hervis, and S. Schwartz. 2003. *Brief strategic family therapy for adolescent drug abuse.* Bethesda, Md.: National Institute on Drug Abuse. NIH Pub. No. 03–4751. Available at http:www.nida.nih.gov/pdf/manual5.pdf.

Chapter 6

Committee on Alcoholism and Addictions, Group for the Advancement of Psychiatry. 1998. *Addiction treatment: Avoiding pitfalls—a case approach.* Washington, D.C.: APPI Press.

Dailard, C. and E. Nash. 2000. State responses to substance abuse among pregnant women. *Guttmacher Report on Public Policy* 3 (6): 3–6, at 5.

Gendel, M. H. 2004. Forensic and medical legal issues in addiction psychiatry. *Psychiatric Clinics of North America* 27:614–19.

Hardy, D. W., M. Patel, and D. Paull. 2000. Basic law for addiction psychiatry. *Psychiatric Annals* 30 (9): 574–80.

Mack, A. H., and H. A. Lightdale. 2006. Forensic addiction psychiatry for the clinician, the expert, and the in-between. *Addictive Disorders and Their Treatment* 5 (2): 80–81.

McKnight, J. T., and J. R. Wheat. 1995. The family physician as medical review officer. *Journal of the American Board of Family Practice* 8 (1): 29–33.

Osterloh, J. D., and C. E. Becker. 1990. Chemical dependency and drug testing in the workplace. *Western Journal of Medicine* 152:506–13.

Sgan, S. L., and R. Hanzlick. 2003. The medical review officer: A potential role for the medical examiner. *American Journal of Forensic Medicine and Pathology* 24:346–50.

Chapter 7

DeWall, C. N., T. W. Altermatt, and H. Thompson. 2005. Understanding the structure of stereotypes of women: Virtue and agency as dimensions distinguishing female subgroups. *Psychology of Women Quarterly* 29:396–405.

Casey, E. A., and P. S. Nurius. 2006. Trends in the prevalence and characteristics of sexual violence: A cohort analysis. *Violence and Victims* 21:629–44.

Chavkin, W., and V. Breitbart. 1996. Reproductive health and blurred professional boundaries. *Women's Health Issues: Official Publication of the Jacobs Institute of Women's Health* 6:89–96.

Cohen, G. H., P. T. Griffin, and G. M. Wiltz. 1982. Stereotyping as a negative factor in substance abuse treatment. *International Journal of the Addictions* 17 (2): 371–76.

Glick, P. 2001. An ambivalent alliance: Hostile and benevolent sexism as complementary justifications for gender inequality. *American Psychologist* 56 (2): 109–18.

Goldberg, M. E. 1995. Substance-abusing women: False stereotypes and real needs. *Social Work* 40 (6): 789–98.

Jos, P. H., M. Perlmutter, and M. F. Marshall. 2003. Substance abuse during pregnancy: Clinical and public health approaches. *Journal of Law, Medicine and Ethics* 31:340–50.

Parks, J. A. 1999. Ethical androcentrism and maternal substance addiction. *International Journal of Applied Philosophy* 13:165–75.

Pollard, I. 2000. Substance abuse and parenthood: Biological mechanisms, bioethical challenges. *Women and Health* 30:1–24.

Resnik, D. B., and R. R. Sharp. 2006. Protecting third parties in human subjects research. *IRB Ethics and Human Research* 4:1–7.

Roberts, L. W., and L. B. Dunn. 2003. Ethical considerations in caring for women with substance use disorders. *Obstetrics and Gynecology Clinics of North America* 30:559–82.

Tillett, J., and K. Osborne. 2000. Substance abuse by pregnant women: Legal and ethical concerns. *Journal of Perinatal Neonatal Nursing* 14:1–11.

Chapter 8

Boonstra, H., and E. Nash. 2000. Minors and the right to consent to health care. *Guttmacher Report on Public Policy* 3:4–8.

Brody, J. L., and H. B. Waldron. 2000. Ethical issues in research on the treatment of adolescent substance abuse. *Addictive Behaviors* 25:217–28.

DHHS (U.S. Department of Health and Human Services). 1983. *Code of Federal Regulations, Title 45: Public Welfare. Part 46: Protection of human subjects regulations governing protections afforded children in research (Subpart D)*. Washington, D.C.: U.S. Department of Health and Human Services.

———. 2001a. *Mental health: Culture, race, and ethnicity; A supplement to mental health: A report of the Surgeon General*. Rockville, Md.: U.S. Department of Health and Human Services.

———. 2001b. *Report of the Surgeon General's Conference on Children's Mental Health: A national action agenda*. Rockville, Md.: U.S. Department of Health and Human Services.

———. 2004. *Surgeon General's Report: The health consequences of smoking*. Rockville, Md.: U.S. Department of Health and Human Services.

Diviak, K. R., S. J. Curry, S. L. Emery, and R. J. Mermelstein. 2004. Human participants challenges in youth tobacco cessation research: Researcher's perspectives. *Ethics and Behavior* 14:321–34.

English, A., and C. A. Ford. 2004. The HIPAA privacy rule and adolescents: Legal questions and clinical challenges. *Perspectives on Sexual and Reproductive Health* 36 (2): 80–86.

Fisher, C. B., and S. A. Wallace. 2000. Through the community looking glass: Reevaluating the ethical and policy implications of research on adolescent risk and psychopathology. *Ethics and Behavior* 10:99–119.

Ford, C., A. English, and G. Sigman. 2004. Confidential health care for adolescents: Position paper of the Society for Adolescent Medicine. *Journal of Adolescent Health* 35:160–67.

Kuther, T. L. 2003. Medical decision-making and minors: Issues of consent and assent. *Adolescence* 38:343–58.

Levy, S., B. L. Vaughan, M. Angulo, and J. R. Knight. 2007. Buprenorphine replacement therapy for adolescents with opioid dependence: Early experience from a children's hospital-based treatment program. *Journal of Adolescent Health* 40:477–82.

Liddle, H. A. 2004. Family-based therapies for adolescent alcohol and drug use: Research contributions and future needs. *Addiction* 99:76–92. Suppl. 2.

National Commission for the Protection of Human Subjects of Biomedical and Behavioral Research. 1978. *The Belmont report: Ethical principles and guidelines for the protection of human subjects of research*. DHEW Pub. No. (OS) 78-0012. Washington, D.C.: U.S. Government Printing Office.

NIAAA (National Institute on Alcohol Abuse and Alcoholism). 2004/2005a. The scope of the problem. *Alcohol Research and Health* 28:111–20.

———. 2004/2005b. Interventions for alcohol use and alcohol use disorders in youth. *Alcohol Research and Health* 28:163–74.

NIH (National Institutes of Health). 1998. *NIH policy and guidelines on the inclusion of children as participants in research involving human subjects: NIH guide notice*. Bethesda, Md.: U.S. Department of Health and Human Services, National Institutes of Health.

Office of National Drug Control Policy. 2007. Drug facts: Juveniles and drugs. http://www.whitehousedrugpolicy.gov/drugfact/juveniles/index.html. Accessed March 8, 2007.

Olds, R. S. 2003. Informed-consent issues with adolescent health behavior research. *American Journal of Health Behavior* 27:S248–S263. Suppl. 3.

Santelli, J. S., A. S. Rogers, W. D. Rosenfeld, R. H. DuRant, N. Dubler, M. Morreale, S. Lyss, et al. 2003. Guidelines for adolescent health research: A position paper of the Society for Adolescent Medicine. *Journal of Adolescent Health* 33:396–409.

Swensen, C. C., S. W. Henggeler, I. S. Taylor, and O. W. Addison. 2005. *Multisystemic therapy and neighborhood partnerships: Reducing adolescent violence and substance abuse.* New York: Guilford Press.

Szapocznik, J., O. Hervis, and S. Schwartz. 2003. *Therapy manuals for drug addiction: Brief strategic family therapy for adolescent drug abuse.* Bethesda, Md.: U.S. Department of Health and Human Services.

Waldron, H. B., and Y. Kaminer. 2004. On the learning curve: Cognitive-behavioral therapies for adolescent substance abuse. *Addiction* 99:93–105.

Waldron, H. B., S. Kern-Jones, C. W. Turner, T. R. Peterson, and T. J. Ozechowski. 2007. Engaging resistant adolescents in drug abuse treatment. *Journal of Substance Abuse Treatment* 32:133–42.

Chapter 9

Alford, D. P., P. Compton, and J. H. Samet. 2006. Acute pain management for patients receiving maintenance methadone or buprenorphine therapy. *Annals of Internal Medicine* 144 (2): 127–34.

Ballantyne, J. C. 2006. Opioids for chronic nonterminal pain. *Southern Medical Journal* 99 (11): 1245–55.

Ballantyne, J. C., and J. Mao. 2003. Opioid therapy for chronic pain. *New England Journal of Medicine* 349 (20): 1943–53.

Breitbart, W., B. D. Rosenfeld, S. D. Passik, M. V. McDonald, H. Thaler, and R. K. Portenoy. 1996. The undertreatment of pain in ambulatory AIDS patients. *Pain* 65 (2-3): 243–49.

Currie, S. R., D. C. Hodgins, A. Crabtree, J. Jacobi, and S. Armstrong. 2003. Outcome from integrated pain management treatment for recovering substance abusers. *Journal of Pain* 4 (2): 91–100.

Geppert, C. M. 2004. To help and not to harm: Ethical issues in the treatment of chronic pain in patients with substance use disorders. *Advances in Psychosomatic Medicine* 25:151–71.

Golden, B. A. 2002. A multidisciplinary approach to nonpharmacologic pain management. *Journal of the American Osteopathic Association* 102 (9): S1–S5. Suppl. 3.

Kahan, M., A. Srivastava, L. Wilson, D. Gourlay, and D. Midmer. 2006. Misuse of and dependence on opioids: Study of chronic pain patients. *Canadian Family Physician* 52 (9): 1081–87.

Langworthy, J. R. 1993. Evaluation of impairment related to low back pain. *Journal of Medical Systems* 17 (3-4): 253–56.

Martin, G., S. H. Ahmed, T. Blank, J. Spiess, G. F. Koob, and G. R. Siggins. 1999. Chronic morphine treatment alters NMDA receptor-mediated synaptic transmission in the nucleus accumbens. *Journal of Neuroscience* 19 (20): 9081–89.

Portenoy, R. K., and R. A. Cruciani. 2007. Pain management in transition. *Advanced Pain Management* 1:2–4.

Public policy statement on the rights and responsibilities of health care professionals in the use of opioids for the treatment of pain: A consensus document from the American Academy of Pain Medicine, the American Pain Society, and the American Society of Addiction Medicine. 2004. *Pain Medicine* 5 (3): 301–2.

Rich, B. A. 2005. The doctor as double agent. *Pain Medicine* 6 (5): 393–95; discussion at 396.

Rosenblum, A., H. Joseph, C. Fong, S. Kipnis, C. Cleland, and R. K. Portenoy. 2003. Prevalence and characteristics of chronic pain among chemically dependent patients in methadone maintenance and residential treatment facilities. *JAMA* 289 (18): 2370–78.

Savage, S., E. Covington, H. Heit, J. Hunt, D. Joranson, and S. Schnoll. 2001. *Definitions related to the use of opioids for the treatment of pain.* A consensus document from the American Academy of Pain Medicine, the American Pain Society, and the American Society of Addiction Medicine. http://www.ampainsoc.org/advocacy/opioids2.htm.

Stewart, W. F., J. A. Ricci, E. Chee, D. Morganstein, and R. Lipton. 2003. Lost productive time and cost due to common pain conditions in the US workforce. *JAMA* 290 (18): 2443–54.

Substance Abuse and Mental Health Services Administration. 2006. *Results from the 2005 National Survey on Drug Use and Health: National findings.* Rockville, Md.: Department of Health and Human Services.

Veterans Health Administration. 2003. Pain management. http://www1.va.gov/pain_management/index.cfm. Retrieved February 10, 2007.

Hazelden, a national nonprofit organization founded in 1949, helps people reclaim their lives from the disease of addiction. Built on decades of knowledge and experience, Hazelden offers a comprehensive approach to addiction that addresses the full range of patient, family, and professional needs, including treatment and continuing care for youth and adults, research, higher learning, public education and advocacy, and publishing.

A life of recovery is lived "one day at a time." Hazelden publications, both educational and inspirational, support and strengthen lifelong recovery. In 1954, Hazelden published *Twenty-Four Hours a Day,* the first daily meditation book for recovering alcoholics, and Hazelden continues to publish works to inspire and guide individuals in treatment and recovery, and their loved ones. Professionals who work to prevent and treat addiction also turn to Hazelden for evidence-based curricula, informational materials, and videos for use in schools, treatment programs, and correctional programs.

Through published works, Hazelden extends the reach of hope, encouragement, help, and support to individuals, families, and communities affected by addiction and related issues.

For questions about Hazelden publications,
please call **800-328-9000**
or visit us online at **hazelden.org/bookstore.**